TO SUSAN,

THE TYPE-Z
GUIDE TO SUCCESS

ENJOY!

Marc Allen

D1009200

ALSO BY MARC ALLEN

Books

The Millionaire Course:
A Visionary Plan for Creating the Life of Your Dreams

Visionary Business:
An Entrepreneur's Guide to Success

The Ten Percent Solution:
Simple Steps to Improving Our Lives and Our World

A Visionary Life:
Conversations on Personal and Planetary Evolution

How to Think Like a Millionaire
(with Mark Fisher)

A Two-Second Love Affair (poetry)

Audio

The Millionaire Course Seminar (3 CDs)

Stress Reduction and Creative Meditations (1 CD)

Visionary Business: An Entrepreneur's Guide to Success
(complete book on 2 audiocassettes)

E-book

The Type-Z Guide to Success with Ease

Music

Awakening

Solo Flight

Quiet Moments

Breathe

Petals

THE TYPE-Z

GUIDE TO SUCCESS

A Lazy Person's Manifesto for
Wealth and Fulfillment

MARC ALLEN

NEW WORLD LIBRARY
NOVATO, CALIFORNIA

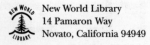
New World Library
14 Pamaron Way
Novato, California 94949

Copyright © 2006 by Marc Allen

All rights reserved. This book may not be reproduced in whole or in part, stored in a retrieval system, or transmitted in any form or by any means electronic, mechanical, or other without written permission from the publisher, except by a reviewer, who may quote brief passages in a review.

Editing: Steve Anderson, Alexander Slagg
Text design and typography: Tona Pearce Myers

Library of Congress Cataloging-in-Publication Data
Allen, Mark, 1946–
   The Type-Z guide to success : a lazy person's manifesto for wealth and fulfillment / Marc Allen.
      p.   cm.
ISBN-13: 978-1-57731-540-7 (pbk. : alk. paper)
1. Life skills—Handbooks, manuals, etc. 2. Success—Handbooks, manuals, etc. I. Title.
HQ2037.A42 2006
650.1—dc22   2005036826

First printing, May 2006
ISBN-10: 1-57731-540-5
ISBN-13: 978-1-57731-540-7
Printed in Canada on partially recycled, acid-free paper

 A proud member of the Green Press Initiative

Distributed by Publishers Group West

10   9   8   7   6   5   4   3   2   1

This book is dedicated to you,
with the hope that you can see
how to create the life of your dreams,
in an easy and relaxed way,
even though you may be lazy, disorganized,
inexperienced, overwhelmed,
or financially challenged.

CONTENTS

PART TWO
Ongoing Course Correction

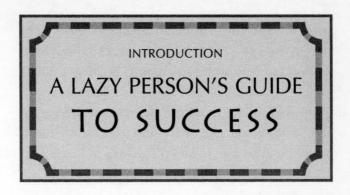

INTRODUCTION

A LAZY PERSON'S GUIDE
TO SUCCESS

You will be as great as your dominant aspiration....
If you cherish a vision,
a lofty ideal in your heart,
you will realize it.

— JAMES ALLEN

I'm lazy. I admit it. For years, it was one of the things that kept me from succeeding in life — after all, you've got to work really hard to succeed, right? That's certainly what I was told, and certainly what I believed.

We call it a *work ethic*: It's good to work, right? It's

1

good for the soul. It builds character. And hard work creates success. But I had a problem with that, if I was really honest with myself, because I didn't want to work all that hard. Given the choice between a day when I have to set the alarm clock and get up early and shower and shave and go to work and a day when I can laze in bed for as long as I want and then do whatever I feel like, I'll take that second option every time.

I've never been a "morning person." It takes me three or four hours to get going, and some days, to be really honest, I never get going at all. Some days I do very little. I've always been that way, since childhood.

"But look at the books you've written," people have said to me. "And the music you've recorded. And you run a publishing company. You can't be lazy and do all that." *Oh yes you can*, I say. All it takes to write a book (or record music, or run a publishing company) is *persistence*.

> You can be lazy and still be persistent —
> and once you learn how to do that,
> you can accomplish a great deal.

Being lazy doesn't necessarily mean being unfocused, unmotivated, and unsuccessful. It's quite possible — it's fairly easy, in fact — to be lazy and still be focused on a goal, and do whatever you need to do, in your own lazy way, to move toward that goal, toward the realization of your dream, step by step.

To many people, the word *lazy* has all kinds of negative connotations. If you're lazy, you're a procrastinator, or you never get started in the first place, or if you do, you're a quitter. It's impossible, most people believe, to be lazy and still succeed. There are very few role models for this, after all. Most successful people seem to have tremendous energy; most of them are Type-A workaholics.

> "You've got to work hard,
> all the time, to succeed."
> That is a deep, core belief
> that is pervasive in our society.
> I decided to challenge that belief, and see
> if it is possible to create success with ease.

I decided almost thirty years ago to try this experiment: I decided to try and be successful — on my own terms, as I want to define success — and yet to do it in my own lazy way (which means I take mornings and Mondays off and never neglect time for long vacations). My experiment was to try and live the life of my dreams, and yet at the same time have a life of ease.

As soon as I tried this, I found something important: When I allow myself to be really lazy for a good length of time, I inevitably find myself full of energy — at least for a while. During these times, it's surprising how much I can accomplish in a relatively short period of time.

On most days, I don't write at all. Some days I'll write for fifteen minutes; some days I'll actually write for a few hours. If you can average a page every other day, in one year you've got a 180-page book.

It took me three years to write my last book, *The Millionaire Course: A Visionary Plan for Creating the Life of Your Dreams.* I put everything I know into that book, everything I learned along the way that changed my life from one of poverty to abundance — and even, more importantly, from frustration and struggle to a pretty startling level of ease and enjoyment (something I couldn't even imagine when I was younger).

But you probably haven't read that book, have you? I can't tell you the number of people who have come up to me and said, "I bought your book, and it's sitting

by my bed, but...I just haven't gotten into it yet."
I've even had people say, "Wow, you've written a 300-
page book! What's it all about?"

In other words, they're telling me they'd never actually *read* a 300-page book, and they want to get the
message in a shorter form. Almost all of us want success, but most of us don't want to work too hard, if
we're really honest with ourselves. I can relate to that
— and so, here's the book that'll show you how to
make some definite, positive changes in your life, *in
an easy and relaxed manner, in a healthy and positive way.*

> **If you *aren't* lazy, you can still benefit
> a great deal from this little book.
> These simple tools work for everyone.**

And if you *are* lazy, you've definitely come to the
right place! I'll make it as easy for you as I can.

> **If you're really lazy,
> just read these bold, centered words,
> and skip the rest.
> You'll get the essence of the book —
> everything you need to create
> the life of your dreams.**

I have a friend and colleague named Ruby. She calls herself "a recovering Type-A workaholic." And she wanted me to add this: This book is not only for lazy people. It's for anyone who wants to succeed, and yet do it in their own unique way.

She says my work appeals to two types of people: Lazy people (like me) and Type-A people (like her) who have worked hard all their lives and would like to relax a bit more now and get off the treadmill of stress and constant work. These simple tools work for anyone who applies them.

HERE'S A LITTLE TALE — a day-in-the-life story. I digress a bit in telling it, so feel free to skip the next two pages if you're really lazy or if you're a Type A and in a hurry as usual to get to the point.

Not long ago I spoke to a loud, enthusiastic group of mostly teenagers. It was a lot of fun. I followed a motivational speaker who had tremendous energy, pacing up and down as he talked. When it was finally my turn to speak, I said something like this:

I fully agree with everything our last speaker said, especially when he stressed the importance of goals, and making challenging goals, and doing what excites you. I say "Amen!" to every word. And I have something to add — maybe it's my one unique contribution to the world — but I have to add this:

> **You can succeed in an easy and relaxed manner.**
> **You don't have to be a Type-A workaholic**
> **to succeed.**

I'm lazy, in fact. No one has ever called me a Type A, or a workaholic. I'm more of a Type Z (as in zzzzzzzzzzz . . .).

A hand shot up. "Are you really lazy?" a young girl shouted out. Yes, I am, I said, and I'm proud of it. "What did you do today?" someone else called out.

No one had ever asked that one before. I had to think about my day for a moment. (I have a terrible memory, as well as being lazy and disorganized — don't ever expect me to remember your name, or anyone else's. In the evening, it sometimes takes me a while to remember what I have done all day.)

Well, I said, it's a Monday, so I took the day off. I always take Mondays off; it's my day to myself. Sundays are for family and rest — and I never do any kind of work on Sunday. Monday is my day for myself, my "mini-retreat."

I slept until about 11:00, laid in bed on my back relaxing until about 11:30. Then I got up and had some coffee and...and I really couldn't remember exactly what I did for the next few hours. A little paper shuffling, I think. Maybe I checked out my stock portfolio on the Internet. At 2:00 or so I went back to bed and laid flat on my back and went through a deep relaxation exercise, and it led to either a silent, calm meditation or sleep, I'm never sure which. (My family claims they hear me snore during my periods of meditation.) Then I showered and left early to drive up to this town so I could hang out in a bookstore coffee shop for an hour or so and have a latte and relax a bit before I had to give this little talk.

That was my day. That's a fairly typical Monday for me, except I almost never have a speaking engagement. I don't do Mondays. I don't do mornings either. I usually work about thirty hours a week in my office (starting sometime Tuesday afternoon), spend about thirty hours a week with my family, and have about thirty hours a week alone, to myself, every week. This is the schedule that works for me.

The high school kids thought that was hilarious — and maybe more than a few of them were inspired just by the *idea*, the *possibility*, that you don't have to work sixty to eighty hours a week at something in order to be successful. Maybe some of them realized something I know is true:

> If I can go from poverty to gratifying success
> in my own lazy way,
> so can you, in your own way.

I don't have any kind of special tools or magic you don't have. We all have a similar brain, we all have the capability to dream and imagine, and we all have doubts and fears. There's no physical difference between a successful person and a poverty case. There is a mental difference, however: Successful people have learned how to focus their creative mind, their imagination, on a goal, and then take the first obvious steps in front of them.

This is no big secret. There are no secrets of success. Every successful person I know loves talking about their successes, and their failures as well. We love to help people out. The only problem is that what we say can sound like a total mystery, like a Zen koan. Or, worse yet, it sounds like something we've heard a million times. It's a cliché. Or it sounds simplistic. Or it directly contradicts something we believe to be true.

Work smarter not harder? What a cliché. Yet many of those old phrases we've heard over and over contain highly valuable keys to success. Working smarter not harder really is a great key — even an essential key — to success. We've all heard it, yet how many of us actually do it?

Most of us are working so hard we don't take the time to work smart. And yet it doesn't take all that much time! It's just a matter of clearly setting goals, and then making clear plans. It takes a bit of imagination — which we all have — and persistence as well, which we either have already or can develop.

I've said it before and I'll say it again:

> **All of us have all the tools
> we need to succeed in life.
> It's just a matter of focusing our creative minds
> in the right direction.**

How do I know this is true? I have to tell you a little story — the story of the day that changed my life.

HOW A LAZY, UNORGANIZED POVERTY CASE BECAME A LAZY, UNORGANIZED MULTIMILLIONAIRE

It was the day of my thirtieth birthday. I woke up in a state of shock, realizing for the first time I wasn't a kid anymore. I was *thirty*. I spent much of the day pacing back and forth in my cheap little slum apartment, thinking about my life — something I had done very rarely in the past.

I realized even back then that I had one great strength, something I was born with — now I see that everyone is born with a unique gift of some kind. The thing I knew in my heart and soul that has served me so well over the years is something a lot of people take years and years to learn, and something some people *never* learn:

> I knew how important it was
> to do what I loved.
> I knew that in some way,
> if I went for my dreams,
> it would all work out somehow.

I could never understand why so many of my friends didn't seem to understand that, and would settle for jobs — and for *lives* — they didn't really enjoy.

I wanted to be an actor and a musician as a child, so I studied music and got into theater in high school. I was in a rock band in high school, too, and then majored in theater in college. (My father wanted me to study business, but I had zero interest in business at the time.)

After college I got a job acting and writing music for a theater company. It was great work for a year or so until the company fell apart. Then I followed my girlfriend to a Zen center in Hawaii, and stayed almost six months before I was kicked out for breaking the rules. (One of the rules was getting up at 5:30 in the morning. Six days a week were highly disciplined, and I had a problem with that. It's amazing to me I lasted as long as I did.)

After that, we tried a back-to-the-land experiment that didn't last very long. Then I wandered around the spiritual smorgasbord of Berkeley, California, for several years, then ended up in a rock band. After a few years, the band broke up, then many months flew by and I can barely remember now what I did all that time — and I turned *thirty*.

I had done what I loved, but I was constantly

struggling to pay the rent, and that wasn't where I wanted to be. I didn't want a life of struggle and stress.

That day, I realized something I had never quite seen before: I realized I had no direction whatsoever. I hadn't been setting the course, or even steering the ship of my life. I had no goals! No wonder I had gone nowhere. I was unemployed, I had no savings whatsoever, no family support, I was *scrounging* (a word we used often) to come up with sixty-five dollars a month rent — in other words, I was a poverty case (two other words we used often).

> I asked myself a question
> I had rarely asked before,
> a simple and important question:
> *What do I want to do with the rest of my life?*

I thought about it for a while, pacing up and down. I didn't even know where to begin. So many possibilities, so many choices.... Then I remembered a little game I had played once in my early twenties during our brief back-to-the-land experiment. We were sitting around a fire one night, and one couple said, "Let's play a little game we played at church camp. Let's imagine five years have passed, and everything has gone as well as we can imagine — what would our lives look like?"

I have no idea what I said when I first played the game — so obviously it had no impact on my life. But I remembered that game the day I turned thirty, and it changed my life.

> I played a simple game:
> I imagined my *ideal scene*,
> five years in the future.
> That little game taught me how to dream,
> imagine, and create.

That day I set my course in life in a way I never had before. The actual mechanics of it were quite simple: I wrote down my *ideal scene* on a single sheet of paper, then I listed all of the goals I could think of on another sheet of paper, then I rewrote each of those goals as an affirmation. Over time, over a few months, plans started to emerge for each major goal — and the next steps to take became obvious.

Of course, as soon as I dared think of my ideal scene and write my first goal, I was filled — overwhelmed — with doubts and fears. Dealing with those doubts and fears became the most important work I did. It took me about five years of constant course correction to reach the first of my major goals — a successful company supporting myself and others — and about ten years to fully realize my ideal scene, which included a spacious and quiet home in northern California, in one of the most beautiful places I have ever seen on earth.

I started my publishing company the day I turned thirty. At thirty-five, I hit my financial low point: My company was nearly bankrupt and I was personally in credit-card debt to the tune of $65,000 (and this was in the early eighties, so in today's dollars we're looking at a substantial sum).

My road to success had been a bumpy, emotional roller-coaster ride, and I had hit the lowest point of my so-called career.

Then three things happened, all about the same time, that quickly turned the company around, so we became profitable and I was, amazingly enough, the debt-free owner of a well-balanced portfolio of investments.

1. I found a way to deal with at least some of my doubts and fears. I went through several sessions, alone with myself and sometimes with others, of what

we call "the core belief process." It's just a simple series of questions that you answer as honestly as you can. (We'll go through it in chapter 3.)

Doing this process led me to realize I had a deep, core belief that I was out of control financially, a fool with money. Then it led me to discover a powerful affirmation: *I am sensible and in control of my finances. I am creating total financial success, in an easy and relaxed manner, in a healthy and positive way.* I kept repeating this affirmation, and it had a powerful effect on my life.

2. I learned about financial controls, and saw they were essential for success. (We'll get into this in chapter 5.) Having financial controls simply means setting things up so you make more than you spend. (This was a new concept for me at the time.)

3. I heard one single phrase that was the catalyst for great change in my life.

> A single simple phrase
> can turn your thinking around,
> and change the course of your thoughts
> and the course of your life.

When I was at my financial low, overwhelmed with problems at work, I heard some inspiring words on the radio that filled me with a strange kind of enthusiasm and, eventually, changed the course of my thoughts. I didn't hear who said or wrote those words — later someone told me it was Napoleon Hill in *Think and Grow Rich*. The phrase is, "*Within every adversity is an equal or greater benefit.*"

I wrote it down in big letters and put it by my phone in my office. Then I added to it, "*Within every problem is an opportunity.*" And later I added a quote from *The Bhagavad Gita*, the five-thousand-year-old spiritual text from India (which goes to show there's nothing new in any of this): "*Even in the knocks of life, we can find great gifts.*"

As I was confronted with problem after problem during this period of struggle and frustration, I started to ask myself, What benefits can there possibly be in this problem? What opportunities? What gifts? And I discovered an amazing thing: When you ask the right questions, you get answers.

The answers come from within you, not from anyone else. Just by asking the right questions, you open up a creative part of your mind that loves finding the solutions to puzzles and problems, even the most perplexing ones. When you ask the right questions, the answers become simple and obvious —

and they're perfectly right for you because they're coming from your own creative mind.

> **This is the visionary idea**
> **that changed my thinking and my life:**
>
> **Within every adversity**
> **are equal or greater benefits.**
> **Within every problem is an opportunity.**
> **Even in the knocks of life we can find great gifts.**

We acknowledge the problems, of course. We certainly can't deny we have problems. But then it's always good to ask ourselves: What benefits can there possibly be for us in this situation? What opportunities? What gifts? Can you see that, just by asking these questions, you open your mind to new, expansive possibilities?

As soon as you begin to look for opportunities, benefits, and gifts in any given situation, you start to find them. Opportunities are everywhere, it's just that usually (especially when confronted with problems) we don't even ask ourselves what opportunities could possibly be right in front of us.

Opportunities are everywhere.
We see them as soon
as we start looking for them.

What opportunities are available to you, right at this moment? Only you know the answer to that, because the answers are in your heart and mind, waiting to be found.

All you need to do is ask.

PART 1

THE FOUR SIMPLE STEPS
TO SUCCESS WITH EASE

CHAPTER 1

THE FIRST STEP
DREAM

Of course you need to build
your castles in the air.
That's where they should be.

— HENRY DAVID THOREAU

The essential first step is to dare to dream. It all begins with a dream. Of course, how could it be otherwise? A dream seems so insubstantial, yet our lives
and our careers are built on dreams; even our
world is built on dreams. As James Allen writes in
his great little book *As You Think*:

"The dreamers are the saviors of the world."

Not only that, they build it in the first place, for everything that has been created was first a dream, an ephemeral idea in the mind of someone who wasn't afraid to consider new and more expansive possibilities.

Without even being consciously aware of it, when I wrote down my ideal scene, I gave my inner dreamer permission to soar.

WRITE DOWN YOUR IDEAL SCENE

The first step is simple. Get a blank sheet of paper or boot up the old word processing program and write "Ideal Scene" at the top of the page. Imagine five years have passed, and you've been so inspired by these words — and by so many other things in your life — that everything has magically gone as well as you can possibly imagine, and you have created the life of your dreams, your *ideal scene*.

What does your life look like? Where do you live? What do you do? What have you accomplished? What does a typical day look like?

Let yourself freely dream. Put all doubts and fears and "realistic" thinking aside for the moment — we'll deal with those later. For now, let your spirit soar. As Steven Covey writes in *The Seven Habits of Highly Effective People*:

"Begin with the end in mind."

C'mon! It only takes a few minutes.

**Take a blank sheet of paper
and write "Ideal Scene" at the top.
Imagine five years have passed,
and everything has gone as well
as you can possibly envision.
What does your life look like?**

What do you do? What do you have? What kind of person are you?

When I did this little exercise the day I turned thirty, I was stunned by the vision that leapt to mind — it was certainly a quantum leap beyond my reality at the time! I imagined I owned a publishing company that was successful and ran very smoothly, publishing books I had written and music I had recorded. I imagined I had a big white house on a hill in a beautiful, quiet place.

I had no idea *how* to achieve this dream. I had no money, and no business experience. I had no idea how I could possibly get from here — poverty — to there — prosperity and success. There were some vague thoughts that some kind of plans must be necessary, but at first I had no idea how to even begin to imagine what those plans would be.

As soon as I dared to imagine this dream, a seemingly endless stream of doubts and fears came rushing into my mind. *That's way too much, Marc. A business? You know nothing about business. And writing books? You've never done that. You're not smart enough. And recording music? That's so much work, and expense. And buying real estate? How can you do that with no money? And you have way too many goals — just pick one thing, and focus on that.*

But I kept turning my thoughts back to my *ideal scene*. Yes, I wanted all of it, a successful business and a lot of time for creative projects and family and friends as well. Not only that, when I really thought about my *ideal*, I wanted it all *in an easy and relaxed manner, in a healthy and positive way.*

Impossible! said my doubts and fears. *It's never*

been done in the history of humanity! I was stumped by that for a while, pacing up and down, but then I stumbled onto a single thought that freed me to follow my dreams.

LOOK AT IT ALL AS AN EXPERIMENT

My thoughts wandered to something I had once heard about the visionary and futurist Buckminster Fuller. I had been told that he came to a time in his life — somewhere in his twenties — when he said to himself that he was either going to commit suicide or look at his life as a completely new kind of experiment. Fortunately for all of us, he chose the latter, and at the end of his life was able to look back on a pretty amazing (and successful) "fifty-year experiment."

I latched on to that phrase, and said to my doubts and fears, *Just give me a year or two to try this experiment: I'll go for it all, for the life of my dreams, and I'll go for it in my own unique, lazy Type-Z way, and see what happens.* My doubts and fears (which seemed a lot stronger than my hopes and dreams at the time) felt it was totally hopeless; I'd obviously fail. *But,* I said to my doubts and fears, *just let me try it, and if I fail, I won't be any worse off than I am right now!*

Even my doubts and fears couldn't argue with that, so I was able to put them aside enough to begin my experiment — to chase after my dreams, in my own lazy way.

Within a year, I had the strong sense that I was on the right path. There were little indications at first, small but encouraging developments, like a check arriving exactly when I needed it, and a friend offering to help in some way. Slowly — in its own perfect time — the company moved forward and started to grow, and I wrote part of a book and recorded some music.

I started to see — and then to believe — that not only was it possible to create success in an easy and relaxed manner, in a healthy and positive way, but that it's the very best way to do it. All our stress doesn't help us one bit; in fact it works against us. The more we relax, the more effectively we do any kind of task.

I had no role models that I could think of. So I looked at it as a fascinating, worthwhile experiment. This little book is a result of that experiment. I'm not asking you to believe me, or to believe in anyone or anything; I'm simply inviting you to try these few simple steps, purely as an experiment, and see what happens.

Does your ideal scene include a life of ease?
If so, make it a priority, and hold
this thought in mind:
It is possible to succeed,
in any way you choose to define success,
and still have a life of ease.

Right now, before you go on, I encourage you to pick up a sheet of paper and write your ideal scene. Just let yourself go, let yourself write whatever pops into your mind. You can always go back later and cross things out, add things, and rewrite. For now, just let your spirit soar.

It's a worthwhile experiment.

CHAPTER 2

THE SECOND STEP
IMAGINE

**First you build your castles in the air,
then you build the foundations under them.**

— HENRY DAVID THOREAU

Did you write your ideal scene? Even if you're really lazy, all it takes is a few minutes. You can do it lying down if you want. You can do it in bed. When I first wrote it down, the day I turned thirty, it probably took less than five minutes.

The next step will only take a few minutes as well.

TAKE THE NEXT STEP

> **It doesn't take much time to work smarter instead of harder.**

Take another sheet of paper, write "Goals" at the top, and list every goal you can think of for the next few years. If you've written your ideal scene, your goals will be right there, in your ideal scene. You've got a picture of where you want to be in five years, now what are the goals you need to reach to get there?

My goals were: *Start a publishing company. Build a successful company. Start writing a book. Complete a successful book. Start recording an album. Record a successful album. Start studying real estate. . . .* (A lot of my goals involved starting things, because I had nothing going at the time.) The first time I did this little exercise I had a total of twelve goals. (Now I'm down to six.)

Let your imagination soar. You've dared to dream of an ideal life for yourself. What goals do you have to achieve to make this happen? Write them down now — every goal you can think of at this moment.

> **Take another sheet of paper,
> write "Goals" at the top,
> and list every goal you can think of
> for the next few years.**

Let your doubts and fears go for a moment. (As I said before, we'll deal with those later.)

> **If you could do, be, or have anything,
> what would it be?**

Without goals, our life has no direction. With goals, our life has direction and purpose. Now that you've made your list of goals, here's a very good question to ask yourself: How can I achieve these goals? How do I get from here to there?

A good place to start is to do the next thing I did on my thirtieth birthday after I wrote my first list of goals. I took another sheet of paper and wrote each goal as an affirmation. The word *affirmation* comes from the Latin root *ad firmae*, which means "to make firm." The right affirmation can be very powerful: When we find an affirmation that works for us, it focuses our creative minds on our goals in a way that, in itself, overcomes a great many of the doubts and fears that naturally arise as soon as we set an expansive goal.

> **Write each of your goals as an affirmation.**

Phrase your affirmations in the present tense, preferably with the word *now* in it. Don't affirm *I will build a successful business* or *I will have a rewarding artistic career*, because the words place your success in the future. Put it in the present: *I am now building a successful business* and *I am now creating a rewarding, fulfilling artistic career*.

> **Make your affirmations in the present,
> as if they're happening now:
> *I am now creating financial
> and artistic success.***

Find the words that work for you. What works for one person may not work for another. Word them positively. Don't affirm, for example, *I am no longer in poverty*. Affirm instead something like, *I am sensible and in control of my finances. I am creating total financial success.*

Keep working and playing with each affirmation
until you find the wording that's best for you.

You'll end up with a list of your goals as affirmations, on one or two pages. (I always try to keep it to
one page.) There are some extraordinarily powerful
words I suggest adding to each affirmation. I discovered these words in a book titled *The Dynamic Laws
of Prosperity* by Catherine Ponder, a Unity Church
minister.

Before or after each affirmation, add the words
*in an easy and relaxed manner, in a healthy and positive
way....* And sometimes, wherever it feels appropriate, add the words, *in its own perfect time, for the highest good of all.*

Keep repeating those phrases, as part of your affirmations: *In an easy and relaxed manner, in a healthy
and positive way, I am now creating abundance in my life.*

Before or after each affirmation,
add these powerful words:
*in an easy and relaxed manner,
in a healthy and positive way....*

I wasn't aware of it at the time, but over the years I have realized that those words overcame a lot of the doubts and fears that inevitably arise whenever we affirm something expansive. *It won't be easy*, whisper our doubts and fears. *It certainly won't be relaxed. Starting your own business or succeeding as an artist is stressful! It may not even be healthy for you. It may not be positive.* Those four words — *easy, relaxed, healthy, positive* — can, when repeated often, have a life-changing effect. These four little words can overcome the paralyzing power of even our deepest and most pervasive doubts and fears.

Many people in our culture don't believe that it's even possible to succeed and still have a life of ease. Or they believe they need to work really hard, maybe even be Type-A workaholics, before they can succeed — and *then* they can relax and have a life of ease.

Many people even equate success with stress: There's a deep core belief that success has to be stressful, that's just the way it is, you have to be a Type A to succeed. I absolutely disagree with this belief (and I'm not the only one!). There are many people who believe exactly the opposite: The more relaxed you are, the more at ease, the more you can and will succeed.

You make better decisions when you've considered everything in a relaxed state. (Everyone knows the value of "sleeping on" something — what can be perplexing in the afternoon is so often simple and clear the next morning.) The decisions we make in stressful states so often lead to more stress; it's the plans we make and ideas we have when we're relaxed that can take our success to a much higher level.

These four words — *easy, relaxed, healthy, positive* — can help you not only achieve your goals, but give you a far better quality of life as you're doing it, starting *now*, this moment.

After I had repeated those words a few thousand times, I could see and feel the changes in my life. I came not to just believe but to realize in my life that *I could succeed in an easy and relaxed manner.* And if I can do it, so can you. It's not all that complex or difficult, either. You take a huge step forward when you simply write down your affirmations and repeat them often.

> **Write a list of goals as affirmations
> and carry it around with you.
> Repeat your affirmations often
> to imprint them on your subconscious mind.**

Write or print out a list of your affirmations and carry it around with you. Read them often. Every time you read them or say them or write them, you are imprinting those powerful words on your creative subconscious mind.

Once you've written your list of affirmations, you'll start getting ideas about the next steps to take that move you toward the fulfillment of your goals. Or you'll hear someone tell you exactly what you need to know at that moment. Or some coincidence will happen that will suddenly propel you a lot closer to your goal. Soon a plan will form, sometimes spontaneously, and you'll discover you can take the next obvious steps *in an easy and relaxed manner, in a healthy and positive way.*

Even if you disagree with many things I say, I challenge you to make a list of affirmations, repeat them often for a few weeks, and *see what happens.*

I believe these principles and practices work not because I made some leap of faith and came to believe them, but because I tried them and saw them working in my life. I had a huge number of doubts and fears when I started taking these few simple steps (consisting of just notes on a few pages of paper!), but I saw remarkable changes in my life in a short time.

Doubts and fears continue to come up, of course. But we can learn to effectively deal with our doubts and fears. This is the next essential step toward creating the life of our dreams.

CHAPTER 3

THE THIRD STEP
BELIEVE

**If you think you can,
or if you think you can't,
you're right.**

— HENRY FORD

We've taken the first essential step. All it involved was writing our *ideal scene* on a single sheet of paper. The second essential step is to write your goals as affirmations.

Have you done that yet? C'mon, all it requires is one or two sheets of paper! And they might just be the most vitally important, even *powerful*, pages you've ever written.

The words you write on those pages become your most important tools for success. Those words guide you, over time, to discover the next steps you need to take. It's very mysterious how it works. You could call it magic, if you like. You can call it anything you want; you can look at it as tuning into your natural, innate creative energy. I like to think of it as modern, effective magic that has had a great impact on my life, in an easy and relaxed manner, for the highest good of all.

> This is a course in magic — modern, effective magic.

It all begins with a dream. First, we dare to dream, and then we give flight to our imagination. Let it soar. What kind of life would you like *ideally*? What goals are necessary for you to focus on in order to get from here to there? We put these goals on paper, and affirm they are now coming into our lives.

Then what happens? As soon as we allow ourselves to dream, doubts and fears come up in almost all of us. The bigger the dream, the greater the doubts and fears. They can seem overwhelming. They cause us to doubt ourselves. They can make us feel foolish for dreaming in the first place. They can make us completely forget our dreams, and settle for lives of dullness and struggle.

THE THIRD ESSENTIAL STEP

The next essential step for almost all of us is to learn how to deal effectively with our doubts and fears. Our own doubts and fears are the greatest stumbling blocks between where we are right now and our highest dreams and most expansive goals.

> **Our doubts and fears**
> **are our greatest stumbling blocks.**
> **Almost all the work to create the greatest success**
> **we can imagine is *inner* work.**

Eckhart Tolle says it simply and clearly in *The Power of Now*:

> **"Get the inside right,**
> **and the outside will take care of itself."**

BECOME MORE AWARE OF YOUR THOUGHTS AND FEELINGS

How do we do this inner work?

First, it's just a matter of *becoming more aware* of our thoughts and feelings. This is a huge step toward

43

changing our doubts and fears: just becoming aware, at every moment, of the thoughts going through our mind.

We don't have to be hopeless victims in an uncaring universe, swept along by uncontrollable currents of thoughts and feelings that overwhelm us. We can easily discover we have the ability to become completely conscious of our doubts and fears; we can learn to observe our minds more closely, to become more aware.

> **We can learn to find *the watcher* within.**

This is a big step toward changing our doubts and fears, and all it involves is becoming more aware of them. For then we discover — not intellectually, but through our physical, mental, and emotional experiences — that our watcher within is coming from a completely different place than our swirling thoughts, our doubts and fears. The watcher is the observer, sitting in a calm, clear place, aware of what is going on, without judgment.

We're naturally calm and clear when we truly observe anything — a sunset, a work of art, a baby's brilliantly shining eyes, our own thoughts. If we have thoughts running in our minds, we don't even see what is directly in front of our faces. In order to see anything, our thoughts have to stop for a moment — and for that moment, we're calm and clear. In that moment, we're receptive, and we see what's in front of our faces with no barrier of thought running through our minds. In that moment, there are no doubts and fears.

Clearly observe your thoughts and feelings. Watch them, without judgment. Watch them come, and watch them go. Most thoughts, even those persistent thoughts, can be gently nudged along. *All right*, you say to yourself, *let that thought go*.

There's a simple exercise that can powerfully affect our lives:

> **When you want to be
> more at ease in the moment,
> just take a deep breath, and as you exhale,
> *let all thought go*.**

Focus on breathing out, if you have to focus on anything, and just for that moment, let all thought go. Even in the middle of a busy day, you can enjoy a moment of stillness.

I do that little exercise many times every day. It simplifies my life, immeasurably. Most of us tend to believe that the problems we face require more thought to solve them. Yet more and more of us have realized that when we let our thoughts go, when we simply relax in the face of a problem and quit working so hard to solve it, simple solutions often emerge, quite easily and naturally. By thinking less, not more, we become more intuitive and even more intelligent.

There's no need to dwell on negative, limiting thoughts. When we realize this, we automatically take another great leap forward in living the life of our dreams:

> **We discover**
> **when we learn to watch our thoughts**
> **that we can *choose* our thoughts.**

We can choose to let those thoughts go that no longer serve us, and we can choose to focus on things that can help make our journey one of ease and fulfillment.

The key is to learn to watch what is going on within us, accept it fully, and let it go. The key is to observe things without resisting them, and then to let them go. Eckhart Tolle sums it up beautifully, again in *The Power of Now*:

> **"To offer no resistance to life
> is to be in a state of grace, ease, and lightness."**

LEARN TO CHANGE
YOUR LIMITING CORE BELIEFS

Over thirty years ago now, I learned a simple little game or process (or whatever you want to call it) that changed my life. The first version of this process was developed by Ken Keyes Jr., author of *Handbook to Higher Consciousness*. Then Shakti Gawain refined the process over several years and wrote it in *The Creative Visualization Workbook*.

> **We can change our beliefs through
> a simple process: the *core belief process*.
> All it requires is for you to be
> honest with yourself.**

There are two versions: the complete process and the short version.

The Complete Core Belief Process

The complete process works best when you're upset about something. You can do it at anytime, around any issue, but when you're upset, agitated, angry, or fearful, it can be a powerful, life-altering experience.

The steps are simple.
Just honestly answer the following questions:

1. What is the problem?

Think of the particular problem, situation, or area of your life you want to improve. Describe it — take two or three minutes to think about it or talk about it in general.

2. What emotions are you feeling?

Name the specific emotions, such as fear, anger, frustration, guilt, sadness. Don't get into any particular thoughts you're having at this point, just pinpoint the single word that describes each emotion.

3. What physical sensations are you feeling?

Explore your body, from your toes to the top of your head. Is there tension somewhere? What is your breathing like? What's going on in your stomach?

4. What are you thinking about?

What's going through your mind? What negative thoughts, fears, or worries are you having? What conditioning or programming can you identify? Take a few minutes to describe your thoughts.

When you do this step, you automatically summon *the watcher*, and begin the process of disassociating yourself from the thoughts going through your mind.

5. What is the worst thing that could happen in this situation?

What is your greatest fear in this situation? If your greatest fear came true, then what would be the worst thing that could happen? If that happened, what would be the very worst thing that could possibly happen?

These questions bring your deepest fears to light. This is a very good thing to do because when you express those deepest fears, you come to realize that the chances of those deep fears actually coming to pass are very slim indeed.

6. What is the best thing that could happen?

What would you like to happen ideally? What is your ideal scene for this area of your life?

You may find this harder to express than your worst fears. If so, your fears may have been dominating and overwhelming your vision of success. Maybe you have been focusing more on the half of the glass that is empty than on the half that is full in your life. Keep the best things, the best possibilities in mind — don't forget your dream!

7. What fear or limiting belief is keeping you from creating what you want?

Now we're getting to the core of the problem: What fear or limiting belief can you identify? Once you've explored this, state your fear or limiting belief as simply and clearly as you can.

It helps to write it down too. If you have more than one, write them all down. Put them in the form of a belief: *I believe that I'm inadequate, that I don't have what it takes....I believe it's hard to make money....I believe my life is stressful and unhealthy at times....*

The simpler the words you use the better. If you possibly can, find words a child would understand. Now we come to the most powerful step of all:

> **8. Create an affirmation to counteract and correct the negative, limiting belief.**

It should be short and simple and meaningful to you, in the present tense, as if it's already happening. *I am enough. . . . I am now creating abundance in my life. . . . I am now creating financial success. . . . I am now achieving my goals in an easy and relaxed manner, in a healthy and positive way. . . .*

Your affirmation is the opposite of your core belief, turning a negative or limiting phrase into a positive, expansive one.

Here's an example: I did this process when I was at my financial low — $65,000 in credit-card debt and on the verge of bankruptcy. I realized I had these core beliefs: *I am a fool with money. I am out of control. I am heading for trouble.* Once I clearly identified those deep core beliefs, I found an affirmation that directly contradicted those beliefs and felt really good to me: *I am sensible and in control of my finances. I am creating total financial success.*

I wrote down that affirmation several times in big letters and put it in different places so I'd keep seeing it and remembering it — by the phone in the office, on the dresser in my bedroom, on the mirror in the bathroom, in my wallet next to the pathetic amount of cash I carried around with me. Whenever those old fears came up, I'd affirm, *I am sensible and in control of my finances. I am creating total financial success.*

After I said it a few hundred (or a few thousand) times, that affirmation began to have an effect in my life. I realized it was not at all difficult to be sensible and in control of my finances rather than to be a fool. It was a choice I was making — previously, it had been subconscious, and now it was conscious.

I kept telling myself I was sensible and in control of my finances, and lo and behold, I became sensible and in control. It wasn't difficult at all to do — in fact, managing my money became very simple. The steps I needed to take were obvious: Spend less than I make. Start saving. Get out of credit-card debt. Start building a diversified portfolio of investments. Get into real estate somehow.

Managing money is not rocket science. Anyone who can do simple math can understand the basics of personal finance. When I affirmed enough times that *I am sensible and in control of my finances,* it became self-fulfilling in my experience.

There's a good lesson in this for many of us:

> **Watch what you say!**
> **The words we tell ourselves are powerful.**
> **Every thought we have has a great deal of power**
> **to shape our entire life experience.**

Here are some more examples of limiting beliefs and affirmations that can overcome those beliefs (many are from *The Creative Visualization Workbook* by Shakti Gawain):

LIMITING BELIEF: *I don't have enough time to do the things I want to do.*
AFFIRMATION: *I have plenty of time to do the things I want to do.*

LIMITING BELIEF: *I have to struggle to survive.*
AFFIRMATION: *I am creating total success, in an easy and relaxed manner, in a healthy and positive way.*

LIMITING BELIEF: *I'm under a lot of pressure at work; it can't be avoided in my high-pressure job.*

AFFIRMATION: *I now relax and enjoy myself at work and accomplish everything easily and skillfully.*

LIMITING BELIEF: *Money corrupts.*
AFFIRMATION: *The more money that comes into my life, the more power I have to do good for myself, for others, and for the world.*

LIMITING BELIEF: *The world is a dangerous place.*
AFFIRMATION: *I now live in a safe, wonderful world.*

LIMITING BELIEF: *It's so hard to have a loving, ongoing relationship.*
AFFIRMATION: *I now have a loving, ongoing relationship that brings me grace, ease, and lightness.*

LIMITING BELIEF: *I don't have what it takes to succeed.*
AFFIRMATION: *I have everything I need, and I'm now creating my own success in my own way. . . . Or: I am now creating the life of my dreams, in an easy and relaxed manner, in a healthy and positive way.*

> **9. Say or write your affirmation repeatedly, over a period of several days.**

Write your affirmation down and put it where you'll see it often. Repeat it silently to yourself, while relaxing, or whenever more doubts and fears come up. Picture everything working out exactly as you want it to.

Shakti Gawain recommends this little exercise, which I'm too lazy to do, but I'm sure would be very helpful: Write your affirmation ten or twenty times a day, if necessary, until you feel you've absorbed it as a positive core belief. If negative thoughts come up, write those thoughts on another sheet of paper, and then keep writing the affirmations on the other page until it feels free of any emotional resistance. In the end, throw away your doubts and fears — shred them and recycle them.

Once you do the core belief process, you'll see for yourself:

> New beliefs can and do replace old beliefs,
> over time, once you have found the affirmation
> that works for you.

That's the entire core belief process. It has worked magic in my life and in the lives of many others as well. Try it yourself — and be prepared for some truly marvelous results.

The Short Version of the Core Belief Process

There's an even easier, simpler way — though the longer version is really powerful when you're upset, as you'll discover if you actually go through it.

The short version is something we can do anywhere, throughout the day: Anytime you feel doubts and fears arising, try to clearly observe them. Acknowledge them, and put them into words: *It's too hard to succeed. This is too stressful.*

Once we can clearly look at our doubts and fears, we can clearly imagine their opposite. Let go of those doubts, with a forceful exhaling breath if necessary, and affirm that the exact opposite of your doubts and fears is now coming into being. *I am now creating success, in an easy and relaxed manner, in a healthy and positive way, in its own perfect time, for the highest good of all.*

> **Whenever doubts and fears arise,**
> **put them into the simplest words you can.**
> **Then find the affirmation**
> **that is the direct opposite**
> **of your doubts and fears,**
> **and say that to yourself instead.**
> **Repeat as often as necessary.**

An affirmation can be very powerful. The right affirmation can overcome years and years — even decades — of limited, negative, doubtful, fearful thinking.

There are many people who believe affirmations don't work. Here is what I've come to believe, based on my own experience:

> **Affirmations are powerful.**
> **Every thought is powerful.**

I've come to realize that it *all* works. Affirmations work. Making goals works. Writing your ideal scene works. Prayer works. Declarations work. Positive thinking works. Auto-suggestion works. Thoughts are powerful things that end up having powerful results in the world.

The problem is that *negative and limited thinking* works as well. Our doubts and fears can become self-fulfilling, if we let them. Our doubts and fears can undo all our affirmations and prayers and positive thinking, if we let them.

Here's how I see it (roughly paraphrasing the way Lenedra Carroll puts it in her great book *The Architecture of All Abundance*): The universe says Yes to every thought we have. Call it what you will — the universe, our subconscious mind, intuition, spirit, presence, God, creative energy, *whatever* — there is a powerful force we are directly connected to, and when we think to ourselves, *I'm going to go for my dream! I'm going to do, be, and have what I want in life!* the universe says *Yes!*, and immediately starts showing us exactly what to do.

If our next thought, however, is *Ah, but it's so hard to succeed... so few people succeed,* then the universe says, *Yes, it's so hard to succeed — for you, with those thoughts,* and then proceeds to show us just how hard it can be.

The universe gives us exactly what we ask for, no more, no less. So ask away. We've heard it said before, so many times:

Ask and you shall receive.

Christ wasn't kidding when he said that. And he didn't say, *Ask and you shall receive if you deserve it.* He said it simply and clearly, so that even a child can understand. And as soon as we understand, deeply, subconsciously, we start receiving what we ask for.

Here is a powerful phrase to add
to the end of your affirmations:

*This, or something better,
is now manifesting
in totally satisfying and harmonious ways,
for the highest good of all.*

So be it. So it is.

We'll end this chapter with what is for me, at least at this moment of my life, the single most powerful poem I have ever read. It's from a little book called *As You Think*, written in 1904 in England by James Allen (no relation to me). I have memorized parts of that book, and the quotes spring to mind often. That little book has changed my life.

Spend a bit of time reflecting on the poem. In the beginning, he means *contentment* when he writes *content*, and he uses the words *environment* and *circumstance* very broadly, to mean anything at all, within you or out there in the world, that you're using as an excuse to prevent you from living the life of your dreams.

You will be what you will to be.

You will be what you will to be.
Let failure find its false content
In that poor word "environment,"
But spirit scorns it, and is free.

It masters time, it conquers space,
It cows that boastful trickster, Chance,
And bids the tyrant Circumstance
Uncrown, and take a servant's place.

The human will, that force unseen,
The offspring of a deathless soul,
Can hew a way to any goal,
Though walls of granite intervene.

Be not impatient in delay,
But wait as one who understands;
When spirit rises and commands,
The gods are ready to obey.

— JAMES ALLEN, *AS YOU THINK*

When you dream of a goal, when you affirm that goal is now coming into being, in an easy and relaxed manner, the creative forces of the universe rush in to support you in moving step by step toward the realization of that dream.

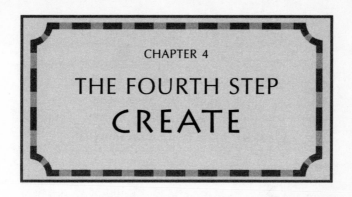

CHAPTER 4

THE FOURTH STEP

CREATE

In the beginning was the Word.

— JOHN 1:1

We've written our ideal scenes on paper, we've listed our goals and affirmed them, and we've begun working with the doubts and fears that arise as soon as we dare to dream.

There's just one more step, the fourth and final step. This one doesn't take that long to do either, and you *know*, while you're doing it, you're working smarter, not harder.

THE FOURTH ESSENTIAL STEP

> Write your plan, for every major goal,
> on one or two sheets of paper,
> and take the next obvious steps in front of you
> to keep moving forward on your plan.

Two things happened in rapid succession as soon as I started to affirm my goals: First, doubts and fears came up in full force, and then, as soon as I had a moment's break from those doubts and fears, plans began to emerge.

Doing the core belief process repeatedly and continuing to say my affirmations regularly helped me deal with at least some of my doubts, fears, and limiting beliefs. I even started to feel on occasion that, just possibly, I might have a far greater potential than I had even dared to dream of. I had a strong sense that I was limited only by my fears and beliefs, and I now had some very good tools to help me deal with those fears and beliefs.

And I discovered what to me is still an extraordinary and exciting fact:

> **Simply writing down your plans
> is in itself a powerful step
> toward the fulfillment of those plans.**

Take a pen and sheet of paper (or pull up your word processing program), put your goal at the top, and write your plan to reach that goal. The whole plan may not be clear at all; perhaps just the first few steps are obvious. That's completely fine. Very few plans emerge at the beginning fully formed. Just write as much as you can at the moment; you can add more later as the plan naturally develops.

My first plans — and most of my plans to this day — had very little structure other than the goal at the top and steps necessary to take to reach that goal. For years, my plans were free-form, unstructured — and effective.

Over the past ten years or so, I've refined the process and sometimes write more structured plans. Use the more structured plans if you want to, but maybe you won't need to. It all depends on you.

I've come to see that the details, the specifics of the plan, are not even all that important: The essential thing is to have a clear goal, in writing, and to have some kind of plan *in writing* to get there, and then to take the next obvious steps in front of you.

Those action steps that you take have results that affect the rest of your plan, and may even change your plan substantially. So don't worry at the beginning about your plan, because it's bound to change anyway. Just start with a plan — *any* plan — and keep changing it and adding to it as you go.

The one element every plan needs is a list of strategies to reach your goal. I use the plural *strategies* because every plan should have a multipronged strategy. Never put all your eggs in one basket; never plan on only one strategy to reach a goal. Have several. Have backup strategies if your first ideas don't pan out.

> Take a single sheet of paper,
> put your goal at the top,
> and list your strategies to reach that goal.

Keep your plan current; keep taking whatever steps you can, and watch what happens. I can almost guarantee you that something will happen that you couldn't possibly plan on that will move you closer to your goal. And it will probably change the course of your plan as well. Update your plan, and take the next obvious steps. The results are magical, in the best sense of the word.

Very few of my plans were fully formed in the beginning. With some, I could just see the next few steps to take. And almost all of my plans changed dramatically over time.

The plan for my business took a few years to write. At first, I could only see the first few necessary steps, which were simply to (1) read a used Business 101 textbook and talk to people who know more about business than I do and learn the basics of business, and (2) get a job, any job, and save 20 percent of my income to finance my first projects.

That was literally all I could think of to do at first. But after I took those steps, the next ones became obvious. After a while I discovered the great benefits of a simple, clear, one-page plan.

> A one-page plan is powerful, because it sets your powerful subconscious mind in motion.

If you want more of a structure for your plan, here are three more possibilities:

1. Sometimes my one-page plans are simply a "To Do" list. I put my goal at the top and then list all the steps I can think of that are necessary to reach that goal.

2. Here's another possibility with a bit more structure. List, in order:

- MAIN GOAL: Your single, overarching goal at the top. You might want to include your mission: your broadest, highest reasons for doing it in the first place.

- GOALS: List the multiple goals you need to reach to achieve your main goal.

- STRATEGIES: The steps you will take to reach those goals.

3. If you want even more structure and detail, here's another option. Four or five years ago, I came across a book, *The One Page Business Plan* by Jim Horan, that suggested the following format.* You

---

* This was amusing (at least to me): I liked the book so much I called Jim Horan and said I'd like New World Library to publish it. He said, "Well, I print those books for ninety cents and sell them for twenty dollars, and I've sold over 25,000 of them on my own — what do I need *you* for?" It was a good question. If you can make $500,000 selling a book on your own, you might as well continue to sell it on your own! He gave me permission to excerpt this bit from his book. For more information, go to www.OnePageBusinessPlan.com.

might have to write very small or use tiny type to get it on one page — two or three pages would be fine as well, because he suggests quite a bit of detail:

- VISION: How do you visualize your company, career, or life in the future? What will it look like in five years? Describe your idea in a way that captures the passion of the idea.

- MISSION: Why do you want to do this? What's your passion? If you have a company, why will customers buy your product or service?

- OBJECTIVES: What are your goals? What accomplishments must you achieve to be successful? List your goals in specific terms, with targets and time frames.

- STRATEGIES: What has made you successful to date? What will make you successful over time?

- PLANS: What specific projects and actions will be taken this year to achieve the objectives?

> Write a brief plan for every major goal,
> and keep your plan current.
> The structure of your plan isn't important.
> Just create your own plan — *any* plan —
> in writing.

Once you have a plan, refer to it often. Take the next obvious steps, and you start to feel your plan gaining momentum. Then you start seeing results.

GET ORGANIZED

Years ago, I told a friend, "I'm completely disorganized." "No," she said, "you're organized where you need to be." I realized that was a much more positive way to look at it, and over the years whenever I find myself looking at the chaos on my desk and think I'm disorganized I substitute the affirmation, *I'm organized where I need to be.*

I've created a simple system to organize my important written material. I have a folder in my briefcase, the kind with flaps inside that easily holds several sheets of paper. The day I turned thirty, I found a folder (with a stunning picture of the Great

Smoky Mountains on it) and wrote these words in big letters on the front: *I am now creating the life I want.* Years later I used just a simple file folder labeled *Magician's Tool Kit.* Now I have a folder with pockets again, with a picture of the earth on the front. At the top I have added a star, and underneath it are the words *I am guided by Spirit every moment.* Put whatever words are meaningful to you on the cover of your folder.

In the folder is my ideal scene, my list of goals and affirmations, and additional notes and other things I've added over time. Keeping this folder at hand and up to date will keep you focused on the essentials. It can become a guiding light in your life, one of your own creation. What a concept — you sit down periodically and, in writing, show yourself where you want and need to go in your life.

The only other things I have in my organized little system are a set of file folders, one for each major goal. My one-page plan is on the top and then I have any appropriate supporting materials, such as mission statements and "To Do" lists, budgets for proposed projects, notes, and whatever else related to that goal I want to keep working with. I keep the set of file folders in my briefcase.

That's my entire little system. It probably took me about ten minutes to set it up originally, after I had written my ideal scene and list of goals as affirmations. C'mon — even a lazy person can find ten minutes. And it's not hard work. It involves no heavy lifting. The only supplies you need are a folder of some kind, a pen, and several file folders.

> **Create a simple system
> to organize this vitally important material.
> Give each goal its own file folder,
> containing your plan and supporting materials.**

If you ever feel stuck — if you feel you're not moving forward toward a particular goal, for any reason — take out your plan and your calendar and write the next step or two you need to take in your calendar, on a specific date. Use your daily calendar to remind you to take the action steps necessary to regain your momentum.

Don't beat yourself up if you don't get around to doing what you've put in your daily calendar. Just move it to another date ahead, and affirm all is happening *in an easy and relaxed manner, in its own perfect time.*

TURN YOUR DESIRES
INTO INTENTIONS

> Once you have a plan in writing
> and take the next obvious action steps,
> you're sending a powerful message
> to your subconscious mind:
> Your dreams and desires
> have become intentions.

Once you have a written plan with your dream at the top, that dream is no longer insubstantial. Once you have written down what you desire and how you plan to achieve it, that desire is no longer fleeting.

As you continue to work with your written plans, a fascinating process is set in motion: Your dreams and desires become *intentions*. An intention is a powerful force; when you intend something, you will make it happen, one way or another. Sooner or later, your intentions will become manifest.

An intention fully engages our conscious and subconscious mind, and draws to it — and creates — support in all kinds of ways we can't possibly plan on, or even imagine. To paraphrase James Allen's great poem quoted in chapter 3:

> You will be what you intend to be.
> When you dare to dream,
> and then make a written plan,
> the creative forces of the universe rush in
> to support you in countless, endlessly creative ways.

Four simple steps are all it takes — so easy to do that even someone as lazy as I am can do them. It doesn't have to take a lot of time or effort. It's just a matter of *focusing your creative mind in the right direction*.

It's worth reviewing — we need repetition to learn new ways of thinking and acting. When you make a plan on paper, you are sending a clear and simple message to your subconscious mind, and to the whole universe and everyone in it: You have a dream or desire for something, and it has now become an *intention*.

You have thought this through, and put it on paper. You are serious; you are going to make it happen, one way or another, sooner or later. You intend on doing, being, or having this, in your own way — and in an easy and relaxed manner, a healthy and positive way, in its own perfect time, for the highest good of all.

> **Clearly state your goal as an affirmation:**
> *I am now creating a successful career.*
> **Put your plan in writing, and then**
> **take the next obvious steps in front of you.**

When you affirm something repeatedly, the universe says *Yes*. And it starts throwing ideas at you: You could start here; you could start there. You could do it this way, or you could do it that way.

Many of your plans develop their own multi-pronged strategies. First you try this, then that, and if those don't work, you go on to another possibility. Sooner or later, you reach your goal, in its own perfect time.

When you put your plans in writing, you unleash or connect with a powerful creative energy, and you start to see opportunities where before you saw only problems and obstacles. You realize there are opportunities everywhere, always, and sometimes you see them and sometimes you don't.

There's a fascinating principle at work here:

> **What we think about expands.**

If our thoughts are focused primarily on our problems and obstacles and shortcomings, those things expand and become even greater. The more we turn our thoughts to what we want to do, be, and have in our lives, the more we let ourselves imagine the life of our dreams, the more those things expand in our lives.

Keep the end in mind. Once your intention becomes solid, solutions to problems become obvious — or else what were formerly problems simply don't matter anymore and become irrelevant. Obstacles dissolve, or else you find an easy, simple way around them.

> **In the simple act of writing
> a one-page plan,
> the blueprint for your success
> is revealed to you.**

Don't let your doubts and fears hold you back. You have everything you need within you to create the greatest success you can dream of. You have a powerfully creative mind — just focus on your goal, and take the next obvious steps in front of you.

If you continue to work with these simple tools, you'll find some wonderfully positive changes in your life. It's up to you:

You are your best visionary mentor
and you are your own worst enemy.
Keep focusing on your dreams and goals,
and you'll reach them in spite
of your doubts and fears.

You have now set your course — the rest is simply course correction.

PART 2

ONGOING COURSE CORRECTION

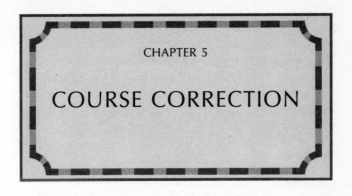

CHAPTER 5

COURSE CORRECTION

We all have a phenomenal mind,
and it includes a direct connection
to a vast subconscious and an intuition
that can guide us every moment.
Now it's just a matter of keeping our powerful
creative minds focused in the right direction.

An airplane is off course over 90 percent of the time.
Yet the pilot keeps correcting, repeatedly, and the
plane arrives at its planned destination.

By taking four simple steps, we have set our
course. Now it's a matter of correcting, repeatedly,
every time we wander off course.

Every doubt takes us off course from our goal —

the realization of our dream. Every argument takes us off course. Every time we're angry, or fearful, or anxious, we wander off course. Over and over, every day, we forget what we know in our hearts to be true. We forget who we are; we forget we have a powerfully creative mind; we forget the unique gifts we have to give to the world.

Over and over, we have to remember to reset our course. When we do that, repeatedly, we will arrive at our destination. It is inevitable. The first and most obvious way to keep on course is to *keep remembering your destination.* It's so obvious — and yet we so often forget, over and over, and need to be reminded of what we know, over and over.

KEEP REMEMBERING YOUR DREAMS AND GOALS

Keep remembering: You are unique and creative. Remember to keep your creative mind focused on your dream, and remember to keep taking the steps necessary to realize that dream.

Don't forget the four steps in this simple program. Don't let doubts and fears cause you to procrastinate, or give up, or never even get started in the first place. Sit down every once in a while and read your Ideal Scene. Update it if necessary. Sit down at least twice a year and rewrite your goals as affirmations. Keep them current, and keep them in mind. (I keep a copy of my goals as affirmations in my back pocket, and pull it out and review it often.)

For every major goal, keep your plan up to date. (It doesn't take all that much time!) The next steps to take will become obvious, and you'll find you can take them in an easy and relaxed manner, in a healthy and positive way, if that is what you've been affirming.

Remember your dreams, always. Remember to have a clear goal for the year. What do you want to accomplish this year? How much income will that create? Did your goals spring to mind when I asked that question? Or did you have to think about it? Keep those goals in mind!

When you wander off course, a great way to get back on course is simply to:

**Remember what you know,
and keep your eye on your destination.**

There are all kinds of other ways to correct your course. Go through these final two chapters and see where you need to pay attention to something and to change something, if necessary.

REFLECT ON YOUR VOCATION AND PURPOSE

So many people have wandered off course for years, decades, even their entire lifetime because the work they have chosen is not appropriate or fulfilling for them.

> **How do we find the right work for us?**
> **Just asking this question**
> **is a step in the right direction.**

Asking that question and trying to find the right answer forces us to work smarter, not harder.

How do we find the right work? It definitely helps to first give some thought to two important facets of our lives: our *vocation* and *purpose*. Once we recognize our vocation and purpose, it helps us focus our creative mind in the direction that leads us to the most satisfying, fulfilling places.

Vocation comes from the Latin word for "calling";

it has the same root as the word *voice*. Your vocation is your calling in life. If you have envisioned your ideal scene, somewhere in that dream of a fulfilling future your vocation is calling to you.

Kent Nerburn said it beautifully in *Letters to My Son*:

Think of work as *vocation*. It should be something that calls to you as something you want to do, and it should be something that gives voice to who you are and what you want to say to the world. It is, above all, something that lets you love.

> Take a sheet of paper and write
> "My Vocation or Calling" at the top,
> then let your spirit soar.

It is, above all, something that lets you love.

Another extraordinarily powerful thing to do — something that can save you years of wandering off course — is this:

> Take another sheet of paper and write
> "My Purpose" at the top.
> Again, let your spirit soar.

You may have difficulty writing even a single paragraph. If so, let it rest for a while, and come back to it. Keep asking yourself what your purpose is. This is a great question to ask, because it forces you to do "big picture" thinking of the highest order.

Sooner or later, you'll find an answer that resonates with the truth that is somewhere deep within you. You may or may not be surprised at what you come up with. Your purpose, expressed in a single paragraph, can become a powerful guiding light for you, helping you make the best decisions, large and small, every day of your life.

James Allen, in *As You Think*, had tremendous insight here:

> **"Until thought is linked with purpose there is no intelligent accomplishment."**

You have a unique purpose for living, and you have been given unique talents and abilities to accomplish that purpose. When you realize what that purpose is, it can help you create a life of magic and miracles.

SEE THE FULL HALF OF THE GLASS AND THE BENEFITS WITHIN ADVERSITY

I have a friend who is smart, talented, energetic — and always struggling to pay his rent. One day he asked me a long, rambling question that I summed up this way: "In other words," I said, "you're asking, *If I'm so smart why aren't I rich yet?*" "Well, yeah," he said. "That's a great question to ask," I said.

I've known him well for years, well enough to know I could tell it to him exactly as I saw it. "Two things immediately come to mind," I said. "On some level — maybe subconsciously — it seems you think you don't really deserve success, for some reason, or maybe you just think it's too hard, or too stressful, to create the life you want.

"Do the core belief process, really look at your deepest beliefs, and come up with an affirmation like, *In an easy and relaxed, healthy and positive way, I am now creating total financial success.* Put it in your own words. If you find the right affirmation, it can overcome all kinds of doubts and fears and get you back on course.

> **Keep repeating something like this**
> **and see what happens:**
> *In an easy and relaxed,*
> *healthy and positive way,*
> *I am now creating total success.*

"What is total success for you? Of course, it's up to you to define it — and the more clearly you define it for yourself, the sooner you'll create it.

"And here's the other thing that comes to mind, as long as you asked for it," I said. "You tend to focus so often on the problems, not on the solutions. You spend a lot of time looking at the empty half of the glass. You often say things are harder than they used to be — there's more competition now, blah, blah, blah — which means you think there's less opportunity now than there used to be.

> **Our beliefs are not true in themselves,**
> **but become true in our experience**
> **if we believe they're true.**

"You can turn your thinking around: It's simply not true that it's more difficult than it used to be to succeed. It only becomes true if you continue to believe it — and a whole lot of people, including me, have a very different set of beliefs. Opportunities are everywhere! They've *always* been everywhere; it's just that we haven't seen them because we haven't been preparing ourselves for them by clearly setting our course."

> You can turn your thinking around
> by asking yourself,
> *What are the opportunities,*
> *benefits, and gifts in the problems I face?*

He got it — I could tell. He had asked for feedback, and I gave it to him as directly as I could. The next time we talked he added one other good thing — something I mentioned at the very beginning: "You know," he said, "as I look back, I can see something else: I've lacked *persistence*. I gave up too soon on some very good ideas, just because I ran into some obstacles. I'm going to be more persistent — and keep remembering to focus more on opportunities rather than the problems."

I've talked to him several times recently and sense a definite positive shift in his energy. The affirmations he has come up with are helping to change those old, limiting beliefs. When he catches himself enmeshed in problems, he challenges himself to find opportunities, benefits, and gifts. And he's being persistent, keeping the same goal in sight until he reaches it.

I have no doubt that, sooner or later, he will realize his dreams — as long as he keeps correcting his course, as long as he keeps remembering and doesn't fall back into the old mental habits that weren't supporting his dreams.

LIVE AND WORK
IN PARTNERSHIP WITH ALL

This is a great key to ongoing success, both business and personal. It's something I've known intuitively for a long time, and something I've done my best to put into practice from the very beginning of my career.

> **The more you live and work
> in partnership with all, the happier,
> healthier, and more successful you will be.**

To this day it still surprises me how many people and how many businesses and corporations, large and small, don't understand this simple concept. Ongoing success is built on a series of win-win partnerships. The more effectively you work in partnership with your family and friends, the greater your personal success will be. The more effectively you work in partnership with your customers, suppliers, and — most of all — employees, the more successful your business will be in the long run.

Not only that, when you live and work in partnership with others, your whole life experience becomes far more enjoyable and fulfilling. I really don't understand why more people don't realize this. It's obvious to me:

> **Partnership is the most powerful form of social interaction that there is.**

If you're not working in partnership with others, you can get way, way off course, and it can become very difficult to get back on course.

I don't understand why more governments haven't realized this: A government has a partnership with every one of its people, and each nation — whether they like it or not — has to work in partnership with other nations if we are to survive and thrive.

I don't understand why more employers don't work in partnership with their own employees, and don't realize, to pick one example, the many benefits of profit sharing with all employees. I split half my profits with my employees. People think this is generous, and that my motives are pure and admirable, but I'm quick to tell them I do it for purely selfish motives — at least for my own self-interest — because I know for a fact that when employees receive substantial profit sharing, they think and act like owners, and we make substantially more profit. Every employee has the power to increase sales or cut costs (or both!), and these things add to the bottom line.

I know for a fact that because I share half my profits with my employees, I make *far more* than twice the profits I would have made otherwise. Most publishing companies have a 5 to 10 percent pretax profit (for the truly clueless like I used to be, this means that five to ten cents for every dollar in sales go to the bottom line on the profit-and-loss statement). Our company makes a 20 to 25 percent pretax profit. I know it's a result of our profit sharing; I see the effects of our profit-sharing program every day I'm at the office.

The numbers don't lie: By sharing half the profits with my employees, we make far more than twice as

much on our bottom line. By sharing generously, I
end up with more. It is one of the finest win-win situations I can imagine.

Profit sharing is an obvious example of the power
of working in partnership. I see the process in action
every week of every year: When a company shares
profits with employees, those employees work harder
and smarter, and those profits expand. Everybody
— owners, employees, and customers — wins in the
long run.

Partnership is based on respect, appreciation,
and mutual support. This is the foundation for any
successful relationship.

> Work in partnership with others
> to help them realize their dreams.
> Then you will have all kinds of support
> for realizing your dreams as well.

Riane Eisler has written masterfully about the effects of working in partnership in her great book
The Power of Partnership. She shows in great detail
and depth that one of the most powerful and rewarding things we can do is to consciously move toward
better partnerships in every relationship in our lives,

including our relationship with *ourselves*, our families and intimate friends, our work and community, our nation, our world, nature, and spirit.

It is a great challenge for all of us to live and work in better partnership with all. Eisler calls it the Great Work, and challenges us all with this sweeping, visionary statement:

> **"This is the Great Work ahead of us:**
> **the reinvention, the re-creation of society**
> **so it is built on partnership**
> **rather than domination."**

We have our work cut out for us. And we can all contribute to this Great Work, each in our own unique and passionate way, by becoming better partners with everyone we know and, indeed, with everyone on earth.

DON'T LET FAILURE STOP YOU

Every successful person I know (including myself) has had his or her share of failures. Look at failure for what it is — at least for what it can be if you have the right attitude:

> **Every failure is an essential lesson
> you need to learn
> along the way to your inevitable success.**

Don't fear failure — look at it as an essential learning tool. Every failure teaches us a great deal; at the very least, it teaches us what *not* to do, and that's invaluable. All the successful people I've known love telling stories of their failures. Our failures are the cost of our real-life education. We learn from our mistakes.

I saw a bumper sticker recently that put it very nicely:

> **Fail 'til you succeed.**

I have a friend who creates magic on a stage, director and playwright John Clarke Donahue. He always comes up with something worth reflecting on every time I talk to him. He recently launched into something like this:

"Why are we so afraid of failure? We should celebrate it! When we can allow ourselves to fail — in small ways, and in huge glorious flops — we're guided on to great things by our creative spirit."

He actually said these words:

"Celebrate glorious failure!"

If you fail, throw yourself a big party and cele-brate! Or at least buy yourself a treat, and give your-self a pat on the back — you went for it, with boldness and devotion. Good for you! Who knows? Next time you may succeed — or the time after that. Don't let failure stop you. Keep going for your dreams.

The only real failure is quitting.

All the other failures are stepping-stones on the way to reaching your dreams.

DON'T DREAM TOO SMALL

This is another way people get off course — or even fail to set their course in the first place: They don't dare to go for that dream they're really passionate about, and settle instead for something far less chal-lenging, more secure, boring, and stifling. They settle for a job rather than a vocation.

It's my job — definitely part of my vocation and purpose — to keep encouraging anyone who will listen to dream the most expansive dreams possible. Start with your *ideal scene*, your greatest dream, and work toward it in any way you can.

Many people simply think and dream too small. If you think small, whatever you create will remain small.

> **Go for your highest dreams!**
> **You'll never regret it.**

I've never known anyone who has gone for their highest dreams and later regretted it. Regardless of what happens, even if it is a spectacular failure, you won't regret it — because you've given your dreams encouragement and support. You have given your spirit a chance to soar. You will find a satisfaction, a fulfillment, beyond anything you've ever experienced.

The great author Goethe had brilliant insight here:

> **"Whatever you can do,**
> **or dream you can, begin it.**
> **Boldness has genius, power, and magic in it."**

It all starts with your dream, so make it an expansive one. When you allow yourself to dream big, and go for it in any way you can, you'll discover you have your own unique abilities — even your own unique genius, power, and magic.

MAKE A DEAL WITH YOUR DOUBTS

I know it all too well from personal experience: The bigger the dream, the more powerful and recurrent the doubts and fears, and they can quickly overwhelm that fragile dream. How can we overcome this very real problem?

I found, simply by trying it, that I was able to negotiate a deal with my doubts and fears. I said to my stubborn inner critic and all those other fearful inner voices: Give me a year or two to try, as an experiment, to go for my dreams — in my own lazy Type-Z style, in an easy and relaxed manner, in a healthy and positive way.

Try it yourself, as an experiment. Give yourself a year or two. Take whatever steps you can in that time, in your own way. Take breaks when you feel like it. Allow yourself to be lazy at times — if you do, you'll find you have a lot more energy at other times.

> Make a deal with your doubts and fears.
> Have them back off for a year or two
> while you try this experiment:
> You'll go for your highest dreams, in an easy
> and relaxed manner, a healthy and positive way.
> See what happens!

Put your doubts and fears aside, purely as an experiment. It worked for me, in spite of all my doubts and fears.

THE THREE ESSENTIALS FOR SUCCESS

In spite of what our doubts and fears have to tell us, becoming successful in business or as an artist is not all that difficult. It's not rocket science or brain surgery. It requires no advanced math, not even a certain level of education.

If you're a parent, you can look at it this way: Parenting is far more difficult and challenging than creating a successful business or career, because in parenting the rules keep changing, and your children keep changing and finding new ways to challenge you. You never know, as a parent, whether you're being too permissive or too strict. It's end-lessly challenging.

Creating a successful business or artistic career is far simpler because it is based on solid principles that haven't changed in hundreds of years. Technology keeps evolving, and the types of problems and opportunities you have keep changing, but the basic rules for success remain ever the same.

There are only three fundamental things you need to have together to create a successful business or career. Each one is essential, however — if you ignore any one of them, it's far more difficult to succeed.

> **There are only three essential things necessary for business and artistic success:**
>
> **1. Find a product or service you love.**

The first thing you need to create success is ob-viously some kind of product or service. The key for true success and fulfillment in this arena is to *find something you love to do.*

This is why it's so good to start with your ideal scene, your highest dream, and keep it in mind as you create your product or service. If you could do anything, what would you do? If money were no object at all, what kind of life would you create?

What do you truly love to do? Start with that question. Do what you love, and the money will follow — and you'll find a satisfaction and fulfillment along the way that is beyond words.

> ## 2. Develop a multipronged strategy to market your work.

Once you've created your product or service, you have to find some way to bring it to market and sell it. The key here is to *develop a multi-pronged strategy* that doesn't take *no* for an answer. Develop a firm intention that, one way or another, you're going to find a way to successfully sell your work.

Here's where a written plan is so valuable: List your strategies to promote and sell your work in writing. Make sure you have several strategies so you always have something else to fall back on if your first attempts aren't successful.

There are countless different ways you can market your work. Get creative. Find out what has worked in the past for others, and do that. If that doesn't work, try something completely new. If that doesn't work, go back and try some other tried-and-true strategy that has worked in the past. If that doesn't work, try something totally off-the-wall, outside of the box.

The comic actor Burt Lahr put it very well:

> **"Keep on the merry-go-round long enough,
> and you're bound to catch the brass ring."**

Sooner or later, if you persist, you'll find something that works.

3. Establish financial controls.

This was the last piece of the puzzle for me to figure out and put in place. With good financial controls, you can be successful with even a very modest level of sales. With poor financial controls, you can blow it at any level of income — even if you're a billionaire (like the Bass brothers in Texas) or a multibillion-dollar corporation (like Enron, which was once the seventh-largest corporation in the United States).

What do I mean by financial controls? I was clueless until, five years after I started my company, we hired a woman named Victoria Clarke to be our bookkeeper. It turned out she brought far more to the business than just bookkeeping skills: She showed me how to make a profit!

Five years after our company was founded, we had a good (and growing) product line and we had some good distributors that were selling our products across the country, even throughout the world, but we were still losing money every month. Victoria whipped our books into shape and then presented me with a single-page report I'll never forget, because that page showed me what financial controls were, and what was necessary to do to implement them.

The page had two columns. The left-hand column had our company name at the top, and under it our income for the past year. Then under that it listed all our expenses during the year in four major categories: Editorial (product development), Manufacturing, Marketing, and G&A (general and administrative expenses, or overhead).

Under each major category, the expenses were broken out further into specific areas. Under G&A, for example, she listed expenses such as rent, utilities, office supplies, etc. Each expense was followed by a percentage figure, which showed at a glance the percentage of our annual income spent on both the large categories of Editorial, Manufacturing, and so on, as well as the percentages for specific expenses such as rent, utilities, office supplies, etc.

The right-hand column was the eye-opener for me: Under the heading "Industry Averages," it listed percentage figures for the exact same categories of expenses. One glance comparing the various categories showed me exactly where our expenses were out of control.

Under Editorial, we were spending roughly 44 percent of our income to develop our projects, compared to the industry average of about 25 percent. Under Manufacturing, we were spending 38 percent of our income, compared to the industry average of 29 percent. Under Marketing, we were spending only 2 percent of our income, compared to the industry average of 11 percent. For G&A, we happened to be spending the same percentage as the industry average, 25 percent.

That single page was like a snapshot showing me our company in a way I had never seen it before. Victoria summed it up by saying, "Here's your problem — you're spending way too much on editorial and manufacturing, and not enough on marketing. G&A is right in line."

It almost felt like a little light bulb flipped on above my head. It was so simple and clear. If you totaled the percentages of our expenses for those four main categories (editorial, marketing, manufacturing, and G&A) our expenses totaled 109 percent of our income, meaning we were losing 9 percent. The expenses in the Industry Averages column totaled 90 percent, meaning the average company our size was making a 10 percent profit.

Over the next few months, we implemented financial controls by cutting our expenses in editorial and manufacturing and boosting our spending in marketing. It wasn't a lot of fun to make those cuts in expenses, but it was essential to the success of the company. Within a short time we became profitable, and have been ever since. (I'm eternally grateful to you, Victoria Clarke — thank you, thank you, for showing me what financial controls were all about.)

We have financial meetings two or three times a year. At the beginning of the year, Victoria presents us with her projections of income and expenses for the forthcoming year, broken out into detailed categories. At the end of the quarter or six-month period, we review the actual expenses for that period against what we had projected. We look at every little expense, and make sure it isn't getting out of line. (Victoria will say things like, "Hmmm...our postage costs have gone from 1.1 percent of our income to 1.3 percent — now why is that?" And we'll sit and discuss postage expenses and see if we've let them get out of control a bit too much.) We are now operating with solid financial controls.

Developing your product, marketing it effectively, and controlling your expenses: Those are the three elements necessary for success. In a larger company, you have different people managing those different functions. But if you're a small start-up company or an individual artist, you may have to handle all three functions yourself, at least for a while.

> **If you have a small start-up company
> or if you're an individual artist,
> sit down a few times a month
> and put on your "marketing hat,"
> and sit down at least every three months
> and establish and review your financial controls.**

In my late twenties, I was in a rock band. When I look back, I scratch my head in amazement that we lasted almost two years, because we had no management whatsoever — no marketing at all, and no financial controls. The only reason we lasted was because we were used to living on very little income.

If I knew then what I know now, I would have sat down with the other band members at least one afternoon a month or so and said, "Look, we've got our product — we're making good music — but we have no manager, so we're going to have to manage ourselves, at least for a while. What do we need to do to manage this band?"

The answer would have been obvious: We needed a plan with a multipronged strategy for promoting the band. The first step would be obvious as well: We had several albums worth of original material; we should record an album, get it manufactured somehow, and have a product to sell wherever we played. And then we should explore other ways to sell our album.

Duh. . . . But I didn't know then what I know now. We had the first of the three essentials — good product. We were doing what we loved. But we had no marketing or financial controls, so we didn't last long.

There's a great saying: Fools never learn from their mistakes, smart people learn from their mistakes, and wise people learn from the mistakes of others. Learn from my mistakes: Get the right product or service, keep marketing it with persistence, and establish financial controls. This is the formula for success.

LEARN AND PRACTICE
THE ARGUMENT-SETTLING TECHNIQUE

I have yet to meet anyone whose ideal scene includes arguments and strife. You have set your course by imagining your ideal life and taking concrete steps toward the realization of your dreams. Along the way, if you find yourself trapped in an argument — whether in a personal relationship or a business endeavor — it's very helpful to realize that argument is getting you nowhere.

As soon as you're in an argument, you can know for sure that you have wandered off course, and need to take steps to resolve the argument before you can get back on course. To put it simply:

> **Arguments are just not an effective way**
> **to communicate.**
> **They do more harm than good.**

No one in the history of humanity has ever stopped in the middle of a heated argument and said, "You know, you're right about that. I changed my mind. I agree with you fully." It has never happened, and never will happen, because as soon as an argument starts, effective communication is impossible.

What happens during an argument? The people on both sides feel angry and frustrated because they're not being heard, and yet neither of them is listening to the other one. As the argument escalates, anger completely takes over and people start saying things they don't even mean. They have essentially reverted to the emotional state of three-year-old children who yell "I hate you!" at their parents because they're not allowed to do something.

Obviously they don't hate their parents — in fact, they love them deeply. But they're angry and frustrated and will scream out hurtful words they don't mean at all. Arguments cause more problems than they resolve.

> **If you get into an argument,
> you can resolve it quickly with the
> argument-settling technique.**

There are two forms of this simple technique: the long form and the short form. Let's go through the longer form first because once you understand the full technique, the short form can be quickly understood.

The Long Form of the Technique

If you find yourself in an argument, go through the following steps:

> **1. Shut your mouth and listen to the other person.**

When you're in an argument, remember this: *This argument is getting you nowhere. Arguing is not going to solve the problem.* The first thing to do is simply to close your mouth, let the other person have their say, and listen.

Do not interrupt them — you'll have your chance to speak next. For now, listen to them without denying what they're saying, defending yourself, or putting yourself or the other person down in any way — not through words, and not through body language either.

Just listen to what they have to say, take it in, and

accept it as being exactly what they need to say to you at that moment. For most people (including me), this is not easy to do at first, but you'll find when you do it that it's a great skill to master, for it not only resolves arguments but greatly empowers you in the process. If you try it you'll quickly understand why.

I've done this process dozens and dozens of times over the past thirty years. This step has never taken more than two or three minutes. Once someone is being listened to, even in the midst of a heated argument, they can say what they need to say in just a few minutes.

> ### 2. Now it's your turn to express your thoughts and feelings.

You've listened to them, without interrupting. Now ask them to listen to you, without interrupting. *That is the key.* They'll have another chance to speak their piece, but now it's your turn.

You'll find it won't take more than two or three minutes.

> ### 3. Now it's their turn to respond. Listen *without interrupting*.

You'll have more chances to respond; but at this point, just listen without interrupting, as you did in step 1. This step rarely takes more than a minute or two.

4. Now it's your turn to respond.

Now you respond. Again, you may need to insist the other person not interrupt you. (If you didn't interrupt them, it's only fair that they listen to you without interrupting.)

These last two steps may have to be repeated several times — let the other person speak, then you speak, without being interrupted. It's rarely necessary to repeat these steps more than two or three times. You'll know when you're ready to move on to the next step.

5. Ask what the other person wants from you.

Listen without interrupting. Every argument is based on the fact that the people involved aren't getting what they want.

6. Tell the other person exactly what you want from him or her.

Be as honest and direct as possible. Make it as clear as possible. Now you're ready for the final step.

7. Negotiate and make clear agreements.

One or both of you may have to compromise in some way, but keep negotiating until you reach an agreement you're both satisfied with. You might have to do some creative brainstorming here and consider a few what-ifs (What if you tried this? What if you tried that instead?), but there will be some creative solution that works for both of you. You will find it if you keep working on it.

The argument-settling technique is simple to explain, but not easy to do at first. When I first did it, I really struggled not to interrupt. In spite of my ongoing affirmation that everything was unfolding *in an easy and relaxed manner*, it was not easy at first. I even used a little notebook and made quick notes of what was said so I could remember to respond to every point. After going through the process a few times, I realized there was no need at all to respond to everything, and notes were completely unnecessary. All that's necessary is to respond to whatever comes to mind, whatever you happen to remember, when it's your turn to talk.

It's all right to make notes, if you want, as long as you keep on listening and don't interrupt — and don't deny, or defend, or put yourself or them down in any way, not even through body language.

The end result is worth it: This simple technique can show you how to live in harmony with other people.

The Short Form of the Technique

There is an even simpler way to use this technique:

> If you get into an argument,
> shut your mouth, stop interrupting,
> and listen to the other person.
> When they're through talking,
> ask them not to interrupt you,
> and speak your piece.
> Repeat as many times as necessary,
> until the argument is resolved.

It sounds almost too simple. But try it and you'll see for yourself: Not long after you start listening to the other person, without interrupting, the anger dissipates. As soon as you start listening to the other, the argument becomes something completely different. To use Riane Eisler's language, we shift from the old dominator model of behavior to true, effective partnership.

Partnership is far more powerful than domination. Discussing problems in a forum where everyone is heard without being interrupted results in far more effective communication than arguments.

There's another way to use this little technique: If two other people are involved in an argument, you can step in and referee, insisting on just one rule: They talk to each other without interrupting each other. You may need to remind them of this repeatedly. But it works every time: You simply cannot have an argument if you sit and listen to each other.

A very powerful thing happens when you discover how to listen to someone, to anyone, without responding immediately, especially without rushing to deny or defend. You become a changed person. You become *empowered* — and those words aren't too strong to describe the effects of this simple process.

CHAPTER 6

THE ONGOING JOURNEY

**The end of all wisdom
is love, love, love.**

— RAMANA MAHARSHI

Maybe this is all too much for you. Maybe you feel overwhelmed at times; there's so much that needs to be done, so many details to handle. Those feelings are common — and they take you off course.

Maybe this quick summary can get you back on course. It's everything I have to say in a nutshell, written for a young friend who is too lazy to read anything longer than half a page or so:

> **The complete course in two sentences:**
>
> **Make a plan for how you can succeed
> by doing what you love to do.**
>
> **Keep doing what you love, and keep taking
> the next obvious steps on your plan;
> somehow, by sheer dumb luck,
> you'll stumble into something that works.**

It's a simple idea anyone can understand: Do what you're passionate about. Make a plan — in writing — that outlines how you're going to be able to succeed doing what you love to do. Take the first obvious steps in front of you. Then see what happens.

Review your plan on a regular basis: Update it if necessary, and take the next obvious steps. Eventually, sooner or later, if you continue trying the next possibility on your plan, you'll find something that works, through sheer dumb luck.

We call it "luck," but we discover when we do this simple process that we have the ability to create it.

> **We create our own luck.**
> **Luck is simply preparedness meeting opportunity.**

When we prepare ourselves — in whatever ways we can at the moment — we become the creative forces that create our own luck. The best way to prepare ourselves is with a written plan. Keep working with your plan, and you'll find opportunities you didn't see before. Eventually, you'll stumble into something that works, and you'll reach your goals, becoming financially successful doing what you love to do.

PRESCRIPTIONS FOR A TYPE-A CULTURE

We all need to get away occasionally, take a break, and forget about work completely for a while. Get some relaxation and recreation. Relaxation has rejuvenating power. It's an essential ingredient for good health.

> **Go on a retreat for a day, a week,**
> **a month if you can, and *relax*.**

Do nothing. Relax. Be lazy. Take a mini-retreat of half a day, or even an hour. Mondays are especially good for retreats — so good that I take almost every Monday as a retreat, a day to do nothing at all, to do whatever I feel like in the moment. I take mini-retreats almost every morning as well.

Think of your home as your retreat center and spa. Relax in your hot tub, if you have one, or take a long hot bath. Relax deeply lying on your back for a while. Get a massage occasionally. Forget your work, forget your troubles. Let go of *all* thought, as much as possible. Enjoy the wonderful feeling of deeply relaxing your body and mind.

Especially if you're a Type A, it's important for your health to balance it by being a Type Z on occasion. If you're a workaholic, look at it this way: When we relax, whether for just brief moments or for longer periods, *the important work is still getting done.* In fact, it's often the best way, the most efficient way, to do the work, in the long run.

> Find little ways to relax throughout the day, especially if your situation is stressful.

There is a simple little exercise all of us can greatly benefit from: Throughout the day, especially in the midst of what seems to be a problem or stress-ful situation, learn to relax for a moment, even for just one breath.

> **During the day, don't forget to relax.**
> **Just take a single, deep, healing breath**
> **and slowly let it go.**
> **Relax . . . and let go of all thought**
> **with your breath.**

Do it now. Do it often throughout the day. Just one breath is all it takes. Two or three breaths are even better. Just let go of your thoughts for a moment, and find that place of silence and peace that is within us all the time, though we're completely un-aware of it when we have a constant stream of thoughts in our heads.

How could it be simpler? Just take a deep breath whenever you remember to, especially in stressful situations. Relax and let your thought go as you exhale.

If you're struggling with an idea or problem, just let go of all thought for a moment. When you start thinking again, you just might have a clearer per-spective on the problem — it might be much sim-pler to find the solution than you thought it was.

You've done an important bit of work in that moment of relaxation.

We all know the value of sleeping on something. So often something that seems problematic in the afternoon is much less complicated, much clearer the next morning. The same thing can happen in a breath, or two or three breaths, for in that brief time a new solution has some room to emerge.

As Eckhart Tolle puts it in *The Power of Now*:

> **"When you are full of problems**
> **there is no room for anything new to enter,**
> **no room for a solution.**
> **So whenever you can,**
> **make some room, create some space...."**

The best thing you can do in the midst of your activity is to relax for a moment and let go of everything, even all thought. Just a single deep breath lowers blood pressure and relieves stress. Just as research has shown that even a minute or two of vigorous exercise can make a big difference in your energy level, even a minute of relaxation can have a calming effect that lasts for hours.

Find short times throughout the day when you

can relax. When you have a bathroom break, you can turn it into a refreshing moment of quiet, letting go of thought.

Sometimes during the day I just lie down on my back and deeply relax. Resting for any length of time is rejuvenating, whether it's for a minute or an hour or anywhere in between. Relax more and you'll stay healthier.*

We used to have a tradition of Sunday as a day of rest, but somehow many of us have lost that tradition. Let's bring it back. After all:

> We all need a day of rest.
> Even God needed a day of rest.

Sunday is a day of rest, prayer, and family for me. I never work on Sunday. And Monday is my day alone, to rest or do whatever I feel like in the moment.

There have been days when I've gotten up, had a strong cup of coffee, and then gone back to bed. My family thinks this behavior is funny. To me it's the most

---

* I know it's self-promoting, but I highly recommend relaxing by quietly listening to my *Stress Reduction and Creative Meditations* CD or my quieter music, such as *Breathe* or *Quiet Moments*.

natural thing in the world. I encourage everyone to relax and nap as much as possible. We can learn a lot from our cats and dogs. A catnap during the day is highly refreshing.

I keep my mornings to myself for sleeping, relaxing on my back, writing, goofing off, being lazy, doing whatever I feel like in the moment. I don't get to the office until Tuesday afternoon, but by then I'm ready to work, energized and enthused.

I take plenty of regular vacations, too — they're important! Don't ever get so busy you forget to take a vacation.

> **Take vacations!**
> **Your soul needs vacations.**
> **They remind us of the important things in life.**

We all need vacations. Our nearly constant activity has to be balanced with some serious laziness every once in a while. And for God's sake, *relax* while you're on vacation. So many people do so much running around in stressful activity on their vacations that they're exhausted when they get home, and need another vacation to recover from their vacation!

When you're on your vacation, practice the fine

art of relaxation, rest, and rejuvenation. Have large blocks of time where you do nothing but relax. Many of us are habitually stressed, even on vacations. Do whatever you need to do to let go of that stress for a while.

When we first work with this material, it involves big-picture thinking and long-range planning. We put our long-term goals and plans in writing, then we take the next obvious steps in front of us. It is essential to make those long-term plans and to keep them in mind. Yet we need to balance all our activity with some stillness, some quiet.

> Dream your dreams as fully as you can,
> and then let them go.
> Balance all your activity
> with some serious laziness.

Here's another thought for all you Type A's out there: Sometimes vacations are the very best things we can do for our business and career. Vacations give our hearts and minds time to reflect on the long-range things that are so vital to us. They can put our lives into clearer perspective; sometimes they can lead to bold decisions and sweeping changes.

Once we have a plan clearly in mind, important work on that plan continues to be done whether we're working away on it at our desk or sitting on a warm beach — and sometimes we make quantum leaps during a vacation that wouldn't have occurred to us at all if we were working as usual.

> **You can have a slower-paced life,**
> **more ease and relaxation,**
> **if you wish; it is up to you.**

From the very first time I imagined my *ideal scene*, an important part of it all was living a life of ease and relaxation — a slower-paced life, with lots of time for my family and for myself as well. What good is having a beautiful home if you're working constantly and don't have time to enjoy it?

Over the years, the personal part of my ideal became much clearer to me, and I realized I wanted to be alone on a retreat a good deal of the time, roughly about a third of my waking hours. To me, it's a perfect balance: I spend about a third of my time in a typical week retreating quietly, another third with my family, and another third in action, reviewing my plans for my various projects and taking whatever steps I need to take next.

This goal has come true for me: I have now realized my dream of becoming a part-time hermit. I have plenty of time alone, plenty of time for meditation, relaxation, sleep, reading, goofing off, and being lazy.

> **This is a call to action:**
> Make your plans, put them in writing,
> and take the necessary steps in front of you.
> And yet this is a call to inaction as well:
> Take time for relaxation, goofing off,
> and being lazy.

I have a few simple rules for my retreats — as with everything else in this book, you may want to completely ignore my rules and make up your own: I am alone. I don't go anywhere. I have no plans. I don't get on the Internet or do email. (I keep my email and Internet access at the office, and don't even have it at home.) I meditate sometime during the day (usually flat on my back), and sleep whenever I feel like it. I write sometimes, and wander around the yard. In the evening I usually take a sauna or hot tub.

After even just a day or two of retreat, I'm always rested, energized, and ready to go wherever I want or need to go — in an easy and relaxed manner, in a healthy and positive way, in its own perfect time.

YOU CAN LEARN TO MASTER TIME

Most of us have heard the old adage that our work expands to fill the time we allot for it. Most of us have seen it happen in our professional lives. We make an assumption about how much time we need to devote to our career, and before we know it our assumption has come true.

We rarely stop to ask if perhaps, like all the rest of our core beliefs, that assumption has become a self-fulfilling prophesy.

> **If you believe you need to work
> sixty to eighty hours
> a week to succeed, or even survive,
> you'll end up doing it.**

To me, that's inhumane. In a typical week, I give my company about thirty hours of focused attention, and that's enough. My work shrinks to fill the time I give to it. When we understand this principle, we can master time.

> **If you believe you can do everything necessary
> to build the success of your dreams
> in thirty hours a week,
> you'll end up doing it.**

To paraphrase James Allen's great poem that we saw earlier: The human will — *that force unseen, the offspring of a deathless soul* — is able to master time, and even conquer space, chance, and virtually any circumstances that confront us.

It is not impossible to master time. It involves looking at our beliefs about time and being willing to change some of those old beliefs. There are many people who have a very different experience of time in their lives, including most of the indigenous people on this earth. Different people have different sets of beliefs about time, and so live in a completely different reality.

Why do people in so many other cultures have so much time to hang out and enjoy life? If they can do it, why can't we? I have a lot of free time by myself to do what I want in the moment — usually more time than I spend at work, in fact — and if I can do it, why not you?

The answer is you can, *if* you're willing to look

at your deeply held beliefs about time. It's odd when you think about it: We all have a large, complex set of beliefs about time, yet we almost never think about those beliefs, and rarely — if ever — examine them consciously. When we do give them some thought, we soon realize that, like all our other beliefs, they are not necessarily true in themselves, but they have a way of becoming true in our lives if we believe them to be true.

By simply looking at our beliefs, and by doing the core belief process when necessary, we discover we can affect those beliefs.

> **We can change our beliefs —
> and our reality changes as a result.**

Until I was thirty-five or so, I believed that there wasn't enough time — or money — in my life. The two were related somehow, and I struggled with both of them. For some reason, God didn't create enough. Time was always passing me by. There was not enough time to do what I wanted to do. I kept noticing that things would always take so much more time than I planned on. Time was flying.

Do any of these beliefs sound familiar?

Then something shifted in my belief system. I found I could make a conscious choice to change my beliefs and create more time in my life. The affirmations I kept repeating somehow had the power to become self-fulfilling — my life experience was now being affected, radically changed, because my affirmations had gained more power, more subconscious strength, than my old, limiting beliefs.

I'm almost certain that the single most effective thing I did was to keep affirming these words with my goals: *in an easy and relaxed manner, in a healthy and positive way, in its own perfect time, for the highest good of all.*

Over time, those words can become self-fulfilling if you repeat them enough.

> **Our entire experience of time shifts**
> **as our beliefs that we have enough**
> **become dominant over our old beliefs of scarcity.**

Are you often stressed, running some kind of race with the clock? What are you thinking, what are you telling yourself at the time? Do you believe there is a shortage of time? Did the universe somehow not create enough for you?

Take a good look at your beliefs about time, and take the necessary steps to change them. Here's the magic formula:

> **Affirm something like this:**
> *My dreams and goals are being realized*
> *in an easy and relaxed way,*
> *in their own perfect time.*
>
> **These words are true magic:**
> **They can help you master time.**

We are slaves to the clock only as long as we believe we are. We are perfectly capable of mastering time. It's a matter of examining and changing our beliefs. There is no universal law that says there is a scarcity of time. We live in an abundant universe, and that includes an abundance of time, money, and everything else.

YOU CAN UNDERSTAND AND MASTER MONEY

Until I turned thirty-five, there certainly wasn't enough money in my life. I had a mass of confused beliefs about money. Money was hard to come by; money was scarce. Money doesn't grow on trees. I believed it took hard work to make money — and when I was honest with myself, I really didn't want to do a lot of hard work. I believed it took intelligence and talent to make money — and deep down I was painfully aware of my stupidity and cluelessness in a whole lot of areas.

It was obvious to me when I looked at my life that I didn't have what it took to succeed. I could barely pay the rent every month, so it was obvious I didn't have enough intelligence or talent to get on top of things financially.

I believed it took money to make money — and since I didn't have any money, the cards were stacked against me. The odds were certainly against me. The rich get richer and the poor get poorer. A fool and his money are soon parted — and when I looked at my history with money, I was obviously a fool.

It was certainly true in my experience: However much I made disappeared almost immediately. Besides, I also felt deep down that maybe money really is the root of all evil. Money corrupts. It is impossible for a rich person to be a good person. As my brother Will put it one time, "Rich people are jerks."

Do any of these beliefs sound familiar to you? It's odd when we think about it: We all have a large, complex set of beliefs about money, yet — just as with our beliefs about time — we almost never think about those beliefs. They're just *there*, unexamined. We very rarely ask ourselves whether those beliefs are valid or really true.

> Our beliefs about money are self-fulfilling,
> like all our other beliefs.
> They are not necessarily true in themselves —
> our thinking makes them so.

Many people think differently, and have very different beliefs about money — which proves that our beliefs are not true in themselves. These beliefs can and do change over time. That has certainly been true in my experience!

Do you believe there is a shortage of money? Did the universe somehow not create enough for you? Do you believe you don't have what it takes to make a substantial amount of money? Do you believe money is hard to get? Do you believe that if you get it, someone else will have to do without it, or in some other way will be hurt by it? Do you believe money will corrupt you? Do you believe it will distract you from the important things in life?

> What are you thinking,
> what are you telling yourself about money?
> Take a good look at your beliefs,
> and take the necessary steps to change them.
> This is the key to mastering money.

Work with the core belief process. Keep saying your affirmations. After I worked with this material for a while, something shifted in my belief system about money and its availability. I came to see and believe that money can be a tremendous force for good in my life, and in the lives of many others. I came to see and believe that I had everything I needed to create the success of my dreams; it was just a matter of keeping my creative mind focused on my dreams by putting my plans in writing and taking the obvious next steps.

> You can make a conscious decision
> to change your beliefs
> and create more money in your life.
> The choice is up to you.

I'm almost certain that one of the most effective things I did in this arena was to ask, to pray — whatever you want to call it — for a specific amount of money, one that was an expansive leap for me to even imagine.

As soon as I ask for an expansive amount of money, I begin to get creative new ideas, and different possibilities come to mind that could very well result in the kind of money I'm asking for. Different opportunities suddenly appear — and it often feels as though those opportunities had been right in front of me all along, but I just hadn't seen them before because I hadn't been looking broadly enough.

Some of the possibilities lead to paths I don't want to take or have no lasting interest in or energy for; some lead to prospects I reject because they don't feel easy, relaxed, healthy, or positive in some way — but some of the possibilities excite something in me, and take me in new directions that are challenging and fulfilling.

Whether we pray for it, affirm it, visualize it, self-hypnotize ourselves, do auto-suggestion or positive thinking or any number of other things, we can come to see and, deep down, *believe* we live in a world that is truly abundant. We can discover endlessly creative ways to create income streams from a wide variety of sources. We will receive what we ask for, no more, no less.

That is a powerful key:

> *Ask and you shall receive.*
> **You receive what you ask for,**
> **no more, no less.**

My entire experience of reality has shifted as newer beliefs gradually replaced my earlier beliefs of scarcity. I don't work hard for money anymore. I do what I love to do and there is always plenty of money. This is what I believe, and this is what has come true in my life. There is an abundance of money in my life, and in the world as well.

Do you have trouble believing this? Maybe it'll help to look at it this way: Money is like food in some ways. In fact, the two are interchangeable. There is plenty of food in the world — in this country, the government pays farmers *not* to grow food. Yet there are people who are starving. There is no shortage of food, but we have a distribution problem.

It's exactly the same with money: There's no shortage of money; there are piles of it all over the world in many different forms — in cash, stocks, real estate, gold, jewelry, art — yet there are many more extremely poor people than there are rich people. Why is this? There is no shortage of money, but we have a distribution problem.

Using the tools in this book, you can discover how to create far more money in your life. And then you can do something in a very real and substantial way to help alleviate someone else's poverty as well as your own.

Henry Ford said it in words that have simplicity, depth, and power:

> **"If you think you can, or if you think you can't, you're right."**

If you can affirm it and believe it, it can become true for you: You don't need to work hard for money anymore. You can do what you love to do and there will always be plenty of money. It's all a matter of your beliefs. If you believe money is scarce, it will be scarce in your life. If you believe there is an abundant amount of money circulating in the world (which there is), it will become abundant in your life.

So be it. So it is!

BECOME A MONEY MAGICIAN

If you still have problems with money after you've been through this whole book, after following this mini-course in manifesting with ease, I recommend you read and work with *Money Magic* by Deborah L. Price. She is an experienced and perceptive financial adviser, and her book's greatest value, at least for me, is the way she identifies the eight possible "money types" (you can probably identify yourself just by her labels) and then shows how to move from our current money type to become the ideal: a money magician.

Do you identify with any of these types of people?

- THE INNOCENT — we all start here; many stay stuck here. Money is a mystery beyond our understanding. We haven't been taught even the basics of saving and investing.

- THE VICTIM — "It's not my fault." Forces beyond my control are always messing me up financially.

- THE WARRIOR — fights and conquers the money world. Often successful, rarely contented or satisfied with that success.

- THE MARTYR — denies oneself for others' needs.

- THE FOOL — gamblers and adventurers who are soon parted with the money that comes their way. (This was me, for years.)

- THE CREATOR/ARTIST — artistic or spiritual, ambivalent toward money, both attracted to it and repulsed by it. (This was my money type as well, from childhood until mid-thirties.)

- THE TYRANT — uses money to dominate and control. Has a life of endless conflict as a result.

- THE MAGICIAN — the ideal — understands how to create money, how to ask for it and receive it.

As Deborah Price says in *Money Magic*:

Using a new and ever-changing set of dynamics both in the material world and in the world of the Spirit, Magicians know how to transform and manifest their own financial reality.

At our best, when we are willing to claim our own power, we are all Magicians. Magicians are armed with the knowledge of the past, have made peace with their personal history, and understand that their source of power exists within their ability to see and live the truth of who they are.

Magicians know the source of power to manifest lies in their ability to tap into their Higher Power. With faith, love, and patience, Magicians simply wait in certainty with the knowledge that all our needs are met all the time.

Magicians embrace the inner life as the place of spiritual wealth and the outer life as the expression of enlightenment in the material world. They are infinitely connected.

> "At our best, when we are willing to claim our own power, we are all Magicians.... Simply wait in certainty with the knowledge that all our needs are met all the time."

If that's too metaphysical for you and you still have money problems, read *Think and Grow Rich* by Napoleon Hill. It is filled with powerful tools to master money.

There is one place where Hill and I part ways, however. He writes (if my memory is correct) that your desire for wealth must become a "single, burning obsession." That sounds to me a bit, well, obsessive. It sounds like something that would get in the way of a balanced and fulfilled life that includes time for family, friends, personal expression, and relaxation as well as making money.

I have seen in my own life that the following simple statement is true:

> **You can create money**
> **and whatever else you want**
> **in a sane and balanced way,**
> **in an easy and relaxed manner,**
> **for the highest good of all.**

There is no need whatsoever to have burning obsessions — clear goals, yes, but not all-consuming obsessions. We can have a balanced life, with plenty of time for rest and relaxation and family, and still create the life of our dreams.

> **Clearly state to the universe exactly what you desire.**
> **Then let it all go,**
> **and let the universe work out the details.**

Go about your day in an easy and relaxed manner, taking whatever steps are in front of you, in their own perfect time, for the highest good of all. Take care of yourself; take care of others. These are the actions of one who understands what is important in life.

THE PURPOSE OF FAMILY

If you're neglecting family and friends, you're getting off course as well. If you're not working in partnership with family and friends, you are definitely off course, and you will be creating endless problems and conflicts.

I have these words written large and posted on my wall:

What Is the Purpose of Family?

To protect and support each one of us,
to be in partnership together,
to respect and love and listen to each other,
to encourage each other to be happy and healthy,
and to help us all fulfill our highest dreams.

This is the purpose and power of family. It definitely helps us stay on course when we remember we are all members of a small, intimately connected family, and we're all part of the great family of humanity as well. We're all stuck here on earth with each other — just as we're stuck with our immediate family, and can't change them or return them for someone else. We're one big, global, dysfunctional family, and we've got to learn to get along with each other without terrorizing each other or dominating and exploiting each other.

The answer, of course, is in partnership. Let's do our best to work in partnership with our family, which includes the family of humanity and all life on earth.

AVOID LAWSUITS

With very few exceptions, lawsuits add to the load of problems rather than create effective solutions. Almost all lawsuits take us off course: They are a foolish waste of time and money, and are completely unnecessary when we work in partnership and learn how to settle arguments.

Our system of litigation is to be avoided at all

costs, because it's a dominator-based system. It is a fight; it is war. The only effective way to resolve fighting (and war) is through mediation, finding creative compromises that work for all parties involved. If you ever have a conflict you can't resolve on your own, find a good mediator and work it out. Mediation is based on partnership.

Our contracts at New World Library have a clause that says any and all conflicts will be resolved between the parties in a spirit of respect and cooperation, with a willingness to compromise; if we can't work it out, we will go to a mediator. If that fails, we agree to go to legal binding arbitration, and resolve it there. Litigation is not an option; hiring lawyers and suing each other is not allowed, because it's a stupid waste of time and resources and simply not the best way to solve the problem.

In nearly thirty years of business, I've never had to go to arbitration. I went to small claims court one time as the very last resort in collecting from a company who owed us for the distribution and sale of our music. It was a simple process that took little time or expense. It involved no lawyers and was a good experience. I've never been involved in any other litigation.

I have used a mediator on one occasion, and it

was a very positive experience for all concerned, a wonderful example of the partnership model. We found a way to get what both of us wanted and yet fully support the other person in getting what they wanted. We came up with a creative solution that was definitely a win-win for all involved.

Living and working in partnership leads to harmony rather than conflict, and the process of mediation resulted in harmony and good feelings — and we continue to this day to work together creatively and enjoyably.

HONESTY AND TRANSPARENCY

For most of you, this section will be obvious. Working in partnership with everyone requires honesty and transparency; they're absolutely necessary ingredients in our ongoing course as we build the foundations of our success through our win-win relationships, whether business or personal.

You know that, don't you?

> Honesty and transparency are absolutely essential
> in working in partnership with everyone
> in your personal life and business affairs.

My wife and I have monthly business meetings. It is just about the only time during the month we talk about money. All our financial dealings are completely transparent: We have our joint account we use to pay the bills, and we each have our separate accounts, and know exactly what the other's holdings are. We never argue about money, because we both have a monthly amount allocated to spend as we will.

What my wife spends her money on is up to her, and vice versa. There are times when she doesn't agree with some of the ways I choose to spend my money — I'm much more of a risk-taker than she is — but we don't argue about it because we each have our own separate pile of money to play with as we choose.

At our last meeting, she told me she was helping out one of her relatives financially. When she explained the situation, I thought I had to include it in here, because it shows another way many successful people go off course, way off course, and even self-destruct.

A couple is married with a child. They have a successful business they both work in. A good portion of the wife's inheritance she received from her family was invested in the business, and it helped their company grow substantially. They have a big house, two nice cars, time to travel, and all the other advantages of success.

The wife is the bookkeeper and, month after month, substantial amounts of cash seem to be disappearing. The husband says he knows nothing about it; his job is keeping the cash coming in, and her job is managing it.

The wife finally finds out — as wives inevitably will — the husband is having an affair, and he's financing his mistress's apartment and other needs. Worse yet, he's been preparing for their eventual divorce by siphoning off cash and stashing it in hidden bank accounts in Switzerland.

When the divorce comes, the husband claims he has very few assets except the house, which he claims is his. He has hired an aggressive attorney, and so the wife has to hire an attorney as well to fight for her rights. It turns into a nasty fight, and soon they aren't even talking to each other, except through their lawyers, which are costing them both an exorbitant amount of money every minute they're involved. (The lawyers bill by the minute. If they spend one minute on a telephone doing something, they bill for a quarter of an hour.)

The attorneys end up making a great deal of money, the business suffers, income drops, and soon both husband and wife are in genuine financial trouble. Worse yet, the husband is completely alienated from both his son and his former wife. They never see each other. He has forfeited all the joys and tremendously satisfying responsibilities of fatherhood.

What is wrong with this picture? It's a lose-lose situation — only the lawyers win (and they win *substantially*).

What if, instead, the couple had worked in partnership, with honesty and transparency? The husband would have disclosed to the wife much earlier that he was having an affair. They could have decided to divorce much earlier, and they could have sat down without lawyers and looked at all their assets and negotiated a fair split. If that was too emotionally difficult, they could have brought in a mediator to do the job.

They could have (and should have) realized that, even if they divorce, they are still partners in their business and will always be partners in child raising. They could have discussed all the options for them in their business partnership: Could one buy the other out? Could they continue working together in some way? Could they sell the whole business?

And they could have made sure their child continued to be nurtured and supported by both of them. It's the child who usually suffers the most in a divorce and yet, if the parents realize they will both always have an ongoing responsibility toward their child, that suffering can be minimized. There's no need for children to lose one of their parents in a divorce. There's no need to punish the child because the parents don't know how to communicate effectively.

With ongoing honesty and transparency, even in a highly emotional situation of divorce and business partnership and parenting, they could have worked out a win-win situation. But the husband's lack of honesty and transparency destroyed everything, including himself. They made two lawyers far wealthier, but it cost them everything.

A wise person learns from the mistakes of others. Look around at the people you know. You can learn a great deal from their successes and failures. In this case, we can learn this valuable lesson:

> **Successful business relationships,**
> **like personal relationships,**
> **are built on honesty, transparency, and respect.**

Isn't it obvious? I don't go around promoting the benefits of honesty, compassion, compromise, and generosity because I'm a good person and these are the qualities of unselfish and caring people. I promote these things because they are absolutely the best way to run a successful business and to create a fulfilling life.

I'm generous for my own selfish purposes. I do it because it helps me take care of myself. It's okay — in fact essential — to take care of Number One, to take care of yourself first. And it just so happens that the best way to do that is by loving and serving others in the best ways you possibly can.

PRACTICE THE 10 PERCENT SOLUTION FOR PERSONAL AND GLOBAL PROBLEMS

You've heard this great key to success before — many, many times. We've all heard it. Why don't more of us practice it?

> **Save *at least* 10 percent of your income.**

The average person in America will make over a million dollars in their working life. Think of it: If you average only $30,000 a year over forty years, you have made $1,200,000. If you save just 10 percent of that, you have a principal of $120,000 — some of it earning interest and dividends and building for forty years!

Saving 20 percent is even better. When I was growing up, our next-door neighbor was a self-employed house painter. We didn't know it, but he was saving 20 percent of the income from every check he received. He retired fairly young, bought a mansion with cash, and was set for life from the ongoing passive income his stocks and bonds generated.

Make it a goal to save 10 to 20 percent of your income. And if you receive some unexpected income from somewhere — bonuses, royalties, windfalls, prizes, or inheritances — save 50 percent of that. Use your savings first to pay off those credit cards, and then to buy your first house, and then to build a diversified portfolio of investments in stocks, bonds, and eventually — if you're so inclined — additional real estate that provides you with rental income. Keep your investments growing by adding to them regularly.

If you save even just 10 percent, it will quickly grow into a substantial amount of money. Then the magic of compound interest happens, and that money begins to make substantial money on its own. You now have a passive income. You are making money with no effort — the very best kind of income for Type Z's!

With regular saving, you become a magician with money.

There is one more aspect of "The 10 Percent Solution" to implement as well — it's also something you've heard hundreds of times:

> **Give away at least 10 percent
> of your income, and you'll change
> your life and the world for the better.**

Again, I am generous not out of the goodness of my heart, but because I know it's the best way to live and to create success. Being generous not only helps others, it helps us as well to grow and become even more successful.

Generosity has a *generative* power — in fact, the two words have the same root word (*genus*, in Latin, which means "to grow, to create family"). To be generous is to generate endless creative energy, energy that comes back to you and supports you and contributes to your well-being in countless ways.

There is a great visionary quote floating around by a writer named Charles Colton:

> **"If universal charity prevailed,**
> **Earth would be a heaven,**
> **and hell a fable."**

Those are wise words, aren't they? If we all practiced charity, earth would be a heaven. As more and more of us support worthwhile organizations working for some good cause, the world more and more becomes a world that works for all of its inhabitants.

The easiest way I've found to save and to donate is to set up three checking accounts: Deposit your income into your general account, then immediately transfer at least 10 percent into your savings account and another 10 percent into your donation account.

Just watch, as soon as you set up clearly in your mind that this is a priority in your life (and setting up separate accounts for saving and donations is a great help), you'll find you're quite capable of living on 80 percent of your income.

You might have a few slips until you really get it, deep within, but you've clearly told your powerfully creative subconscious mind that saving and giving are priorities in your life. Your subconscious says *Yes*, and shows you exactly how to do it, easily and effortlessly. It might include finding new streams of income; it could involve simplifying your life in some ways and cutting expenses.

> Save 10 percent and give away 10 percent.
> You are on your way to financial independence —
> and you're helping out others along the way.

Just imagine: You have consciously become part of the solution rather than unconsciously being part of the problem. Congratulations!

RETIRE FROM THE RAT RACE

> Here's a great question for you:
> How can you kick back, relax,
> and yet do what you love successfully?

Why not look at it this way?

At a certain age, all of us want to retire from the rat race, get off the treadmill, take it easy.

Type Z that I am, I've wanted to take it easy all my life. Now that I'm in my late fifties, I'm at an age where most people would agree with me that it's time to start relaxing more. But even throughout my twenties and thirties, there was always a voice in me that wanted me to relax and slow down and not work so hard all the time.

I wanted to do things with ease and lightness — that became obvious to me the minute I first thought of my ideal scene. And at some point along the way, I began to see that having ease and lightness in my life was not dependent in any way on outer circumstances — *it is an inside job*. The ease I wanted was up to me to find; it will never be something that I will achieve once I do something necessary out there in the world, like build my income to a certain level or buy my dream home or have the perfect wife and 2.5 children.

> **Having ease and lightness in your life is an inside job.**

That simplifies things immeasurably, doesn't it? We don't have to do anything else in the world before we can relax throughout the day. We don't need anything else at the current moment before we can have a life of ease and lightness.

The rat race is all in our mind.

Why not look at it this way? We have created the rat race ourselves; *it is all in our mind.* We create our own stress, usually subconsciously. All we need to do is some *inner work*: Let's decide to retire from the rat race, and choose to live our lives with more ease and relaxation.

We can do this at any time, at any age. So you might as well decide to retire from the rat race *right now*. Why not? Congratulations! You have decided to retire from a life of stress and choose instead to kick back and enjoy life, doing what you love to do as much as possible. Wonderful! Give yourself a pat on the back for retiring at the youthful age of _____ (fill in the blank with your current age).

Just by making this internal decision, the external world will follow. Keep affirming your goals are being met, *in an easy and relaxed manner, in a healthy and positive way,* and you'll see great changes in your world.

Maybe not all of your goals and dreams will

come to pass. I've affirmed many, many goals and dreams over the years that haven't come into being. Yet some of them did and do come into being. The perfect ones, in fact, when I think about it. This is certainly a wonderful key:

> **The goals and dreams that are perfect for you are the ones that finally come true.**

Dream big. Dream in multiple directions if you feel like it. Some of your dreams will come true — the perfect ones for you.

So be it. So it is!

LOVE, SERVE, AND REMEMBER

I have a friend in Boulder, Colorado, who works for two people who deal with money and investments in ways I can't even understand, even when he carefully tries to explain to me what they do all day. But I learned one very important thing from him: He said he loves working there because the owners have one main goal in their work: They just want to be "guided by Spirit."

Every morning, I walk outside my beautiful home.

First I simply quiet my mind for a few moments, then I say a little prayer of thanks. I always try to mention something I haven't thought of before, because the list of things I'm grateful for is infinite, including every cloud in the sky, every cricket, every blade of grass — the endless variety and evolution of life itself.

I ask to be guided by Spirit, and then I quiet my mind again...and Spirit speaks. The words are almost always the same: *Love, serve, and remember.*

Remember what? *Remember who you are: a spiritual being having a physical experience. Remember your connection to Spirit, always. Relax! Breathe deep. You are guided by Spirit.*

Remember to serve. Remember Tagore's beautiful poem:

> **I slept and dreamt that life was joy.**
> **I woke and found that life was service.**
> **I acted, and behold! Service became joy.**

Most of all, remember to love. This is the most essential thing, after all, in the teachings of Jesus. "A new law I give unto you: Love one another." Love your neighbor. Love even your enemies. Love and forgive everyone — they know not what they do.

Above all, love the Creator, in whatever way you choose to describe the great mysterious forces that brought you and your world into being.

Ramana Maharshi, one of the world's greatest guiding lights of the last century, said what is in my opinion probably the single most profound and important sentence ever expressed by a human being:

> "The end of all wisdom
> is love, love,
> love."

Love and serve everyone, all humanity, including yourself. Love and serve your Mother Earth and the wildness of nature. Love and serve the divine within you. It is guiding you in the same way it guides the galaxies.

When you love and serve, every decision you make is for the highest good of all. You are guided not only to the greatest success imaginable, but to the most fulfilling and satisfying life possible, in an easy and relaxed manner, in a healthy and positive way, in its own perfect time, for the highest good of all.

The greatest keys for success in your career and in your life can be summed up in these few powerful, life-altering words:

> **Love and serve.**
> **Remember these words,**
> **and you'll always stay on course.**

ACKNOWLEDGMENTS

I'd like to thank everyone I've ever met over the years who has so generously contributed their time, their expertise, their dreams, their support. Whenever I really need advice or help, it appears.

The entire list would turn this into a very boring thousand-page monster, but I'd like to especially thank:

Eckhart Tolle, for walking your talk, living with grace, ease, and lightness, and for writing the book that lightened my life, *The Power of Now*;

Shakti Gawain, for our ongoing creative partnership, and for writing *Creative Visualization*, the book that launched our company;

Victoria Clarke, for helping this dreamer get his feet on the ground, and teaching me how to run a profitable enterprise;

Munro Magruder, who so capably supplied the essential piece of the puzzle of marketing and selling our work, helping the company to grow;

Ruby Yee, for her visionary leadership and enthusiasm about my work;

Sky Canyon and Robert Powell, for years of creative partnership, musical and otherwise;

The staff of New World Library and everyone at Publishers Group West, our excellent distributor: I couldn't have done it without you; and finally,

My wife, Aurilene, for her unwavering faith and support, and Giselle and Kai, for lighting up my life.

ABOUT THE
AUTHOR

Marc Allen has been a lazy Type Z all his life. In his twenties, he was a financially challenged actor and musician. He was fired from several jobs, including busboy and dishwasher (for being too slow) and typesetter (for not showing up on time and taking too many breaks).

The day he turned thirty, with no financing or business experience, he started a publishing company that he built, in his own lazy way, into a highly successful business. Along the way, he managed to write several books, including *The Millionaire Course, Visionary Business, A Visionary Life,* and *The Ten Percent Solution,* and record several albums of his music, including *Breathe, Petals, Quiet Moments, Solo Flight,* and his latest, *Awakening.*

Originally from Minnesota, he lives with his family in northern California.

For more information about his books,
audio projects, or seminars, go to
www.MarcAllen.com or www.SuccessWithEase.net.

For information about his music,
and to sample selected tracks,
go to www.WatercourseMedia.com.

This book is now available as an innovative e-book called *The Type-Z Guide to Success with Ease*. It features animation, audio segments, and even a relaxing slide show with wonderful music to give you a break from your busy day.

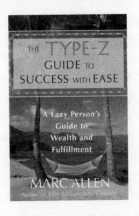

To check out a free sample chapter
or to order, go to:
www.SuccessWithEase.net/FREEChapter

NEW WORLD LIBRARY is dedicated to publishing books and other media that inspire and challenge us to improve the quality of our lives and the world.

We are a socially and environmentally aware company, and we make every attempt to embody the ideals presented in our publications. We recognize that we have an ethical responsibility to our customers, our employees, and our planet.

We serve our customers by creating the finest publications possible on personal growth, creativity, spirituality, wellness, and other areas of emerging importance. We serve our employees with generous benefits, significant profit sharing, and constant encouragement to pursue our most expansive dreams. As members of the Green Press Initiative, we print an increasing number of books with soy-based ink on 100 percent postconsumer waste recycled paper. Also, we power our offices with solar energy and contribute to nonprofit organizations working to make the world a better place for us all.

Our products are available
in bookstores everywhere.
For our catalog, please contact:

New World Library
14 Pamaron Way
Novato, California 94949

Phone: 415-884-2100 or 800-972-6657
Catalog requests: Ext. 50
Orders: Ext. 52
Fax: 415-884-2199

Email: escort@newworldlibrary.com
Website: www.newworldlibrary.com